In *Hurling's Top 20*, bestselling author and broadcaster Colm Keane profiles 20 of the greatest hurling legends to grace the game: from Christy Ring, Mick Mackey, Jack Lynch and Tony Reddin to more recent heroes such as Nicky English, Joe Cooney, Brian Whelahan and D.J. Carey.

Tipperary's John Doyle and Jimmy Doyle, Kilkenny's Eddie Keher and Noel Skehan, along with Cork's Ray Cummins and Jimmy Barry-Murphy recall their glory years.

Offaly's Joe Dooley together with Wexford's Billy Rackard and Tony Doran describe how their counties beat the odds, turning the tables on the traditional hurling powers, while Waterford's glory years in the 1940s and '50s are recalled through career profiles of John Keane and Tom Cheasty. Jimmy Smyth describes Clare's fallow years.

Hurling's Top 20 chronicles over half a century of hurling history, as seen through the eyes of those who have played at the highest level of the game. Incorporating amusing anecdotes, first-hand match descriptions and behind-the-scenes analysis, *Hurling's Top 20* is a must for hurling fans.

For Seán

MAINSTREAM SPORT

HURLING'S TOP 20

COLM KEANE

MAINSTREAM
PUBLISHING

EDINBURGH AND LONDON

Reprinted 2006
This edition, 2003

Copyright © Colm Keane, 2002
All rights reserved
The moral right of the author has been asserted

First published in Great Britain in 2002 by
MAINSTREAM PUBLISHING (EDINBURGH) LTD
7 Albany Street
Edinburgh EH1 3UG

ISBN 1 84018 775 1

A catalogue record for this book is available from the British Library

Typeset in Berkeley and Gill Sans Condensed

Printed in Great Britain by
Cox & Wyman Ltd

Contents

INTRODUCTION

LONG BEFORE THE ERA OF THE CELTS, THE ANCIENT SPORT OF HURLING HAD ITS FOLK heroes. Years before Christ, pre-Celtic warriors fought for supremacy with a ball and stick. Perhaps no better symbol can be conjured than the ancient warrior hurler, exhausted from honest endeavour, scarred, bloodied from battle, proud in victory or defeat. Perhaps it meets our need to establish tribal rankings, to settle differences, to generate potent symbols of superiority and power. Maybe it's our urge to celebrate exceptional skill, to idealise qualities of strength and agility. Either way, from the early mists of time, hurling heroes have settled differences on the field of play rather than on the field of battle.

No doubt our ancient ancestors struggled, as we do, to establish the hierarchy of hurling giants. Almost certainly, arguments raged over which sporting warriors displayed the finest talents, the greatest courage, that unique ability to dominate games. Great Titans have stood out in every age and still do. However, those deserving of the highest accolade of greatness are notoriously hard to select.

Unfortunately, there are no definitive measuring devices for establishing the credentials of legendary hurling stars. Medals and trophies alone are clearly insufficient given the enormously talented individuals who played with unsuccessful counties. Had a player like Jimmy Smyth of Clare lived in nearby Tipperary or Cork, he might now have five, six or even seven All-Ireland medals to show for his hurling endeavours. Instead, despite his enormous talent, he ended his career with none.

Neither could Christy Ring or John Doyle have accumulated their record eight All-Ireland medals without the depth of hurling talent that surrounded them. Imagine Christy Ring's Cork without Paddy Barry,

Willie John Daly, Josie Hartnett or Mattie Fouhy! Imagine John Doyle's Tipperary without Mick Roche, Pat Stakelum, Tony Wall or Liam Devaney! Great sides foster and support great talents. They also generate a store of winners' medals.

There are, however, some simple measures for establishing greatness in sport: exceptional skills, ability to take control and to influence the outcome of events, strength on the playing field, unselfishness, longevity in the game and concern for fellow players all form part of the test. Often, those attributes combine to produce extraordinary medal collections. It is no coincidence, for instance, that the 20 hurlers selected in this compilation won over 70 senior All-Ireland hurling medals between them. One player alone, Noel Skehan, won nine senior All-Ireland medals, six from the field of play.

More often than not, those who watched them play, or who played with them, point to an indefinable aura of stardom. They describe their ability to light up a pitch by their presence, the buzz of anticipation when they home in on goal, their ability to read a game and to turn a match at crucial moments with rare displays of talent. Those are the qualities described, time after time, by witnesses to the early days of Jimmy Doyle, Jimmy Barry-Murphy, D.J. Carey and Nicky English, amongst others. Destiny, it was clear, would treat them well, as it did in a succession of All-Ireland finals.

Ultimately, the selection in this publication is a subjective one, the product of hundreds of conversations with former and current players, officials, supporters, commentators and observers of the game. Few of their proposed lists concurred with one another; there always were deviations based on age and county affiliation, amongst other factors. As one might expect, all hurling fans have their special favourites, many of them relatively obscure performers who caught their attention and won their respect for purely personal reasons.

Universally agreed, however, was the right of all those selected to be counted among hurling's all-time legends. It was quite remarkable how unanimous the consensus was. Strong cases were made for other great players but then who might be dropped to make way for their inclusion? At day's end, all those covered in the pages ahead have made unique contributions to the game, brightening playing fields with their skills, bringing joy to those lucky enough to have seen them play, while inspiring younger generations to emulate their achievements. Such is the mark of greatness.

Inevitably, there are many people to thank for their help in compiling this publication. My gratitude to Helen Shaw, Director of Radio in RTÉ, for her role in getting this project up and running. Helen, as always, provided the maximum encouragement and support. Thanks also to Fionnuala Hayes, of RTÉ, for transcribing the sound interviews with her usual care, dedication and efficiency. I am also grateful to Noel Roberts, of RTÉ, for his expertise and patience in compiling the radio programmes.

Many people, all of them great hurlers or eminent GAA dignitaries, unselfishly shared memories of the legends featured in this book. Among them were Pat Fanning, Andy Fleming, Frankie Walsh, Austin Flynn and John Barron of Waterford, Con Murphy and Willie John Daly of Cork, and Dick Stokes of Limerick. Mick Dunne, of RTÉ, conducted the fine interview with Jack Lynch that formed the basis of the Cork legend's chapter. Jack's wife, Máirín Lynch, was gracious with her time and her enthusiasm for the project.

Scores of people, in dozens of counties, also offered their guidance and advice. None was more helpful than William 'Nooche' Kenefick, from Youghal, a one-time player and lifelong supporter of hurling. The gang at Bertie Dempsey's pub in Youghal also provided a steadying hand, despite the nature of the trade. Paddy Glackin, of RTÉ, helped devise the initial short-list. Nioclás Mac Craith, of Ring, County Waterford, steered me in the right direction with some of the Irish derivations and spellings. Ned Keane, of Villierstown, County Waterford, along with Donal Cullinane and Willie Coleman, of Cork, also provided invaluable support.

Thanks also to Tommy Barrett, Jim Forbes, Paddy Dunphy, Pat Dunphy, Jimmy Hartigan, all of various GAA County Boards, for their direction and their contacts. Owen McCann went to considerable trouble to help with the chapter on Eddie Keher. Anne Kearney with the *Irish Examiner*, Jim Carney with the *Tuam Herald*, and many others too numerous to mention, pulled out all the stops with the photo illustrations. My gratitude for the cover photo to Norman from Inpho. Also, to Barbara Durack, Joan, Rob and Ian at various RTÉ archives, and especially to Margaret-Mary O'Mahony at the RTÉ Stills Library, my thanks for all the help.

For the launch of this book, William Kenefick enlisted the help of many in the town of Youghal, County Cork. It's the home of some great Cork hurlers, including Willie Walsh, Pat Hegarty, Seánie O'Leary, Brendan Coleman and many others who contributed to the game throughout the years. Denis Murphy, Liam Gleeson and Brian Gleeson were an enormous help. Thanks also to the Mayor and elected members of Youghal Urban District Council. Others in the town, too numerous to mention, will know of my gratitude.

Bill Campbell and Peter MacKenzie of Mainstream, together with all their staff, were great to deal with, as was Lorraine McCann. Their enthusiasm and efficiency made this project pleasant to work on. Also central was Úna O'Hagan, who read the raw chapters, provided untold hours of advice and always offered support, while Seán Keane's interest in hurling and involvement with Bray Emmets provided the initial impetus for the project.

Finally, I would like to thank all the contributors for their efforts in compiling this publication. All were generous in giving of their time and imparting information, with some sharing stories and recounting tales of great matches from eras long gone by. Relics of their greatness, in the form of medals and other memorabilia, survive in museums around the country. But, as photos fade and bits of silverware become tarnished, tales and recollections of their skills linger on as fresh as ever. Hopefully, some of their golden moments have been captured in the following pages. Like their greatness, their memories deserve to last forever.

Colm Keane
August 2002

1. JACK LYNCH

THUNDER AND LIGHTNING BOOMED AND CRACKLED AT THE ALL-IRELAND FINAL IN 1939.
The heavens opened, spilling a deluge of rain on the 40,000 spectators.
Great peals of sound and bright flashes of light enveloped the ground.
The crowd was soaked. The players struggled to hold their footing on
the rain-sodden turf. The dye from their shirts ran onto their shorts.
Players were obscured in the poor visibility. It was a miserable scene,
never before or since witnessed at an All-Ireland final. Inevitably,
history would refer to it as 'the thunder and lightning final'.

That September afternoon, clouds of a more ominous nature hung
over Europe. On the morning of the match, Neville Chamberlain
announced Britain's declaration of war with Germany. The previous
Friday, German troops had spilled into Poland. Dáil Éireann met in
emergency session to discuss Éire's response to the crisis. The hum of
conversation was of war more than hurling. The weather was
appropriate to the mood of the day.

For two hurling counties there was work to be done on that day in
September 1939. Cork and Kilkenny were battling for the
championship in a repeat of the 1931 decider. Back then, Cork had
won. In 1935, Kilkenny had secured their last success. Now, the two
great counties struggled with an unprecedented deluge to secure
another All-Ireland crown. Togging out for Kilkenny was the future
legend, Jimmy Langton. The captain of Cork that day, in time, also
would achieve legendary status. Leading the Rebels in his first All-
Ireland final was the future Taoiseach and subsequent winner of six
consecutive All-Ireland hurling and football medals, Glen Rovers' Jack
Lynch.

'It was one of those days that we will remember for a lot of reasons,'

Jack Lynch told RTÉ's Mick Dunne in a comprehensive radio interview. 'The main reason is that it had been Cork's first final since 1931. They had been looking forward to it for a long time. We were hoping that this was the breakthrough. I don't think Cork had been out of the All-Ireland final in hurling for as long ever before in their history. A few of our team went to see Kilkenny play Galway in the semi-final and thought we were well over them. We went out certainly with an air of confidence if not with complacency.

'We were brought out to a hotel in Monkstown the night before in order to get us away from the madding throng, to the Salthill Hotel, now no longer in existence. The following morning, we went to mass in Monkstown parish church and it was lashing rain. We went on to Croke Park then. It was still raining. During the course of the day, the sun came out brilliantly, hailstones fell and we had thunder and lightning.

'It was a raging storm and the rain came down like stair-rods. At times, in some parts of the pitch, it was very hard to see more than about 20 yards away from you. Being the first Sunday in September, with rain coming down so heavily, the ground wasn't able to absorb the heavy fall of rain. The ground conditions themselves were very difficult. We were a bit strange in the sense that we hadn't been to Croke Park before, at least not as a senior inter-county hurling team. Kilkenny had been there already, many times, and they seemed to settle in much more quickly.

'They took us rather by surprise in the first half. I remember it for a lot of instances myself. Towards the end of the game, I got a little push from behind; I think it was Jimmy Kelly. I was about to tackle Paddy Phelan. With the push in the back, I fell in on top of him and a free was given against me. The free was taken by Paddy Phelan himself and it went right into the goal and was about to pass the right-hand upright, as one looks towards the goal. Batt Thornhill told me that Seánie O'Brien just knocked it over the line and the umpire gave a seventy.

'Then, to add to the problem, the seventy was taken and three of us got under it. The ball was heavy and didn't get in very near the goal. It was maybe 15 to 20 yards out. Jim Young was on my left. I was directly under it and Jack Barrett was just ahead. I shouted to Barrett: "Okay, I have it." Barrett mustn't have heard me, or else didn't trust me. But he leaned back, with the result that he almost overbalanced, got his stick to it and barely touched it out to I think it was Jimmy Kelly. The three of us pounced on him but, of course, he just got it through for a point. That was the winning point. We were convinced there were a few more minutes left but they weren't played. We were beaten by the proverbial one point by Kilkenny.

'I believe Mr de Valera called a special meeting of the Dáil either that morning or the day before. I remember some of my former TD colleagues mentioning that the meeting was over soon enough to come to Croke Park. We hadn't had war since 1918. That was 20 years before. I suppose nobody expected there would be a repetition of the 1914–18 war. But then the catastrophe did happen somehow and did impinge on our minds afterwards because it made hurling and travelling to hurling matches very difficult. One thing it caused for us was a cancellation of a tour to America, which we were to be given whether we won or lost. In fact, none of that Cork team ever got to America on a tour.'

Throughout the war years, Jack Lynch was an automatic selection for the Cork senior hurling team. Born in August 1917, he had arrived on the inter-county scene via his club, Glen Rovers. Since fifth year at the North Mon, he represented the county seniors. In the latter half of the 1930s he played with a county that was underachieving. Having failed to reach a Munster final in six consecutive years, Cork, in the middle to late 1930s, were living in the shadows of Limerick, Tipperary and Waterford. All that, however, would soon change dramatically.

In the first half of the 1940s Cork embarked on an odyssey that would never be matched in hurling history. From 1941 to 1944 they won a historic four-in-a-row All-Irelands. They hammered Antrim in one of those finals. In the others they beat a Dublin team fleshed out with country hurlers arriving as part of the emergency forces. 'They were one of the top teams,' Jack said of Dublin. 'At that time, there was a big influx of army personnel. In fact, some of the army personnel we played against were Corkmen.'

The Cork revival began in 1939 with victory over Limerick in the Munster final. More battles with that great Limerick side would ensue in subsequent years. Those contests would pitch players like Limerick's Mick Mackey and Dick Stokes against Cork's Christy Ring and Jack Lynch. Other matches involved Waterford's John Keane and Andy Fleming, and Tipperary's Tommy Doyle.

'My greatest memories of those were our games against Limerick, in particular, who were almost at the peak of their best in those days,' Jack recalled. 'We had some tremendous games with Limerick in the early '40s, memorable games. I always remember many a tussle I had with Mick Mackey. When I was asked to comment on his death, I did mention that he always gave it tough and took it, and he'd hit you hard. If you were fool enough to be in the way, that was your business. There was always a kind of smile on his face when he was doing these things.

'I think the attendances were very high. I often passed scores of fellows on the road from Cork to Limerick, and Cork to Thurles, and when I was living in Dublin, from Dublin to Thurles. A funny thing in those days was that participants were entitled to travel in a taxi but nobody else. I remember driving from Dublin to Thurles in a taxi all by myself and some of my friends, my colleagues on the Civil Service hurling team, many of them Cork people, were cycling. I passed some of them around Portlaoise and there I was sitting in my glory. It was a silly thing. There was no reason why they shouldn't have sat in with me if I was permitted to go.

'Especially during the war years, most of us had to travel by bike. It used to be a great excuse in those days, of course, when you'd go to a match and you might bring a girl to a match, and you'd kind of say, of course, with the petrol situation we have to use the bike. But we all went training, night after night, cycling. Some of the distant fellows came by car. These were hired cars mainly. I don't think any member of our team owned a car.

'We cycled to many a game, not so much with the Cork team but many a club game. I remember one time getting a lift on the crossbar of a bike out to Ballincollig to play a game. When I got off the crossbar I thought I had no leg. I had to soften out. There was a great commitment. That's not to detract from the young fellows nowadays. There must be commitment because they're producing. No matter what they say, they're producing a high quality of hurling and football.

They are probably fitter than we were. However, I'd like to see that tested.

'We had a very good team. It was a good all-round, balanced team. You can't say we hadn't stars when we had people like Christy Ring, John Quirke and Jim Young. But there were no outstanding stars. No one man seemed to be any better than the other men on the team. I think the biggest asset that team had was that when inevitably some people had an off day we used to be able to find some reserves. It might be Jim Young one day, John Quirke another day, Christy Ring another day, Willie Campbell, Alan Lotty. There were always one or two men who would do something to lift the whole team. This was, I think, the strength of that team.'

Of the names associated with the Cork four-in-a-row team, few, apart from Jack Lynch, could compare with Christy Ring and Jim Barry. Although both contributed to the side's success, they couldn't have come from more different ends of the hurling spectrum. Christy was the rising young player from Cloyne who was overshadowed by the established stars on the team and was yet to be fêted for his genius. He would, in time, win eight All-Ireland medals. Jim Barry was the legendary trainer whose involvement with Cork led to four titles in the late 1920s and early '30s, the four-in-a-row in the '40s and the three-in-a-row in the '50s.

'No, he wasn't,' Jack replied when asked by Mick Dunne if Christy Ring was as dominant then as he became in the 1950s. 'One would expect that a man in his very early twenties would have come to his best. I wouldn't presume to say that he was probably playing with better men when he was at his best. But I think it is true in his case that he probably matured, although I don't know if you could say that Christy Ring matured because he was a hurler since the day he was born. But he probably got more experience and was able to read the game better. His reputation was building up during our time. Therefore, I suppose, there were a lot of factors, psychological, experience and otherwise, that made him the dominant character in the '50s.

'Jim Barry had a tremendous ability to bring out the best in the team he was training. He used to do everything. When the training session started, he used to go down to the park, as we used to call it, it's Páirc

Uí Chaoimh now, to make sure that the grass was cut. If it wasn't, he'd kick up holy murder. He'd make sure that the jerseys were washed and the towels were washed.

'If somebody was working, perhaps it might be a traveller or it might be somebody on shift work and therefore his job would take up time when he should be training, Jim would go to the boss, the managing director, and insist that this man be let off. After matches, win or lose, he always made sure that the team was sitting down to a good meal. He wouldn't let anybody interfere with the welfare of the team in any respect.

'Jim was generous. He hadn't a lot of money but I know that he made what little he had available to the people who were in trouble from time to time. When I say trouble, I mean just ordinary financial embarrassment, temporary financial embarrassment. He had a lot of characteristics that made one like him and respect him. All these put together, particularly his enthusiasm, tended to bring the best out of the team.'

Not even Jim Barry could inspire the Cork hurlers as they pursued a fifth All-Ireland in a row in 1945. In fact, they bowed out as early as the Munster semi-final, where they lost to Tipperary. With that defeat, the Cork hurlers' hopes of securing a fifth All-Ireland medal in a row disappeared. Not so, though, in the case of Jack Lynch. Although football was his second favourite sport, he qualified with Cork for the 1945 All-Ireland football final. There, Cork beat Cavan to win their first title in 34 years, while also securing medal number five for Jack Lynch.

'I was doing my Bar final that year, in '45,' Jack recalled. 'I was in digs in Dublin, near Terenure, Brighton Road, which wasn't far from the 16 bus route. It went right beside Croke Park, down under the railway bridge along the road out in Drumcondra. I met the team in the hotel in Dublin the night before and I usually foregathered on the morning of the game for a cup of tea and maybe a pep talk. I said to Jim Barry: "I don't think there's any need for me to come in. I'm living only 30 yards from a bus and I'll go out and get the bus. I'll be around in good time."

'I did that. I went to the bus queue near Kenilworth Square. Several buses passed and there was a big queue and I was getting a bit worried.

I was looking at my watch. Of course, it didn't occur to me at that time to get a taxi. I was surprised. I thought there should be no attraction in Dublin with the football final. I was surprised that so many people from that area seemed to be going to the football final. I suppose many of them were going about their own business otherwise.

'After a while, when I got really worried, I broke the queue and stepped on the platform of the bus. The bus conductor put up his hand: "Oh, nothing doing. You have to take your turn." I said: "Listen, I'm playing in the All-Ireland football final today." "Ah," he said, "that's about the best one I ever heard. Stay on." I think the story was such a good one he decided to give in to me.'

For Jack Lynch, it was back to business with the Cork hurlers the following year, 1946. A Munster final clash between Cork and Limerick promised much but delivered little. Cork won easily, following which they defeated Galway in the semi-final. They also took control of the All-Ireland final, defeating Kilkenny by the remarkable score of 7–5 to 3–8 before a crowd of 64,000. That victory brought Jack the unique distinction of being the only player in history to win six All-Ireland medals in succession.

'We had a very good team that day and we won it well,' Jack said. 'Ring, of course, was just coming to the height of his fame. I think that was the day he got a tremendous goal from about halfway in, one of the most spectacular solo runs ever seen in Croke Park. All round, it was a very good display. Perhaps Kilkenny were taken by surprise or were probably not as good as they were the following year. But, strangely enough, even though it was my sixth in a row I wasn't terribly conscious of that fact until later. I had appeared in Croke Park in an All-Ireland final in almost every year during that decade. I wasn't really conscious about the six-in-a-row until I read about it afterwards.'

There was one other record achieved by Jack Lynch that, along with his six-in-a-row, would stand the test of time. It occurred on Sunday, 20 February 1944, when he played in three games in the course of one day. In the morning he appeared for his club, Civil Service, in the Dublin league. That afternoon he togged out for Munster in two Railway Cup semi-finals. The first was the hurling semi-final against Ulster, won resoundingly by Munster. The second was the football semi-final against Ulster, which Munster narrowly lost.

'I had been playing with the Civil Service and I was picked for the Munster hurling and football teams,' Jack recalled. 'I was, as they say, doing a line at that time and my wife, which she is now, Máirín, said: "What are you going to do today?" "I suppose," I said, "I ought to go to Croke Park, and I don't think I'll play in the morning with the Civil Service." She said, even though she wasn't a typical GAA man: "Well, surely your club comes first?" And I said: "Goodness, you're right."

'I went out to Islandbridge and it was a funny saga in a way because they asked me if I was going to play and I said I would. But I said: "Would you mind if I played in goal?" They said: "Not at all, but we might want you out the field later." I went to the goal for the first half. There were five balls came my way. There were three goals, one point and one wide in the first half. I decided that it was time to give up any aspirations I might have to be a goalkeeper.

'We had no tracksuits in those days, except to pull my trousers up over my togs, and my jacket over, and dash to Croke Park, just change jerseys and go out with Munster. We played the hurling first that day. We won that fairly well. I think it was against Ulster in both. The football, we were doing very well. I changed jerseys but just changed numbers rather than the colour. I remember well a ball coming across towards the end of the game and we were about a point or two down. Somebody passed it from the left corner in to me and I was coming in. I had to run fairly fast to get it and I got near it. But I honestly hadn't the energy to kick it. If I had, it would have been an easy goal.

'I decided that day that never again would I play three matches in the one day, nor would I advise anybody else to do so. Even though I was fairly fit in those days, there's a certain amount of fatigue. I often wonder how tennis players play for four hours on end. I suppose there's more bodily contact in GAA games and I suppose that knocks the stamina out of a person as well.'

Throughout his career, Jack Lynch won eleven county championships with Glen Rovers, with eight of them won in a row. He also added National Hurling League and Railway Cup medals to his record six senior All-Irelands in succession. A Texaco Hall of Fame award-winner, he was selected on both the hurling Team of the Century and the Team of the Millennium.

While still playing hurling and football, he was elected to Dáil

Éireann in 1948. By then, he was in his thirties and his time as a sportsman was running out. He lasted two more years as a hurler, formally retiring in 1950 following Glen Rovers' successful defence of their county title. Then, in 1952, he played his very last hurling game, appearing for a hybrid émigré Cork team in New York.

'It was a competitive game but nothing to do with the GAA in Ireland,' Jack says. 'I was part of a parliamentary delegation to a conference in Ottawa in 1952 and I had played my last hurling game in 1950. I came back via New York. I met a great friend of mine there, Paddy Barry, who was a former Glen Rovers hurler. Paddy suggested to me on the Saturday that I might go to Gaelic Park. Cork were playing the next day. I said I'd love to go.

'I went up and there were a lot of other games as well, probably two or three other games. The first game was almost coming to an end and the Cork game was about to start, and they asked me to come in and meet the team. I met them and they said: "Well, why not tog out with us and play?" I said: "It's two years now since I've played." I had put on a bit of weight. They pointed to a fellow in the corner: "Sure, look at him, he's about forty." I was about early thirties at this time. "He's nearly a grandfather." So, after more persuasion, I said: "Yes, I'll line out for ten minutes."

'Having fulfilled my contract, I lay down after ten minutes. They said: "Keep going. We might have a chance." They didn't expect to win it. I said: "Okay, another ten minutes." It went on and on until half-time. They then said: "Listen, if you go off now, you know, we're right in the game, the wind is behind us . . ." I said: "Okay, I'll stay on."

'In the last couple of minutes, anyway, I hit a ball. I was playing centre half-back, I think, and probably had no more than about 60 yards to hit the ball from that position. I was watching it. It was going for the goal and I wanted to know if it was going wide, or barely wide, or barely inside. Just as the ball was about to land, I got a charge with a hurley in the ribs. That was at least two seconds, I suppose, from the time I hit it. I went down in some pain.

'The following day, I came back. I had flown out and I decided I would come back by boat for the experience on the *Nieuw Amsterdam*. It was the flagship of the Holland–America fleet. It was a small boat by Atlantic liner standards and it happened to be a very rough crossing.

The good old ship was tossing around and every movement it made I was getting a bigger pain in my ribs. Eventually, I went in to my bunk and I asked if the ship's doctor would come. I don't think he was a very highly qualified man. But, fair play to him, he did diagnose broken ribs and he put one of those two-inch gauze bandages around me and gave me a shot of some morphine, or something like that, which was not nearly strong enough.

'I was tossing around in the bunk all that night and until I landed in Cobh. When I woke up the next morning I was really hurt because the gauze bandage had rolled itself into a kind of whipcord and I was cut to pieces as well as being sore inside. That was the last hurling match I ever played and I know I'm hardly likely to play one like it again.'

At the time of Jack Lynch's New York visit in 1952 his political career was already overshadowing his hurling success. A Parliamentary Secretary since 1951, he soon acquired a succession of ministerial portfolios, including the Gaeltacht, Education, Industry and Commerce and Finance, before being elected Taoiseach in 1966. He served as Taoiseach from 1966 to 1973 and from 1977 to 1979.

Although his political duties increasingly focused his attention on national affairs and on political life in Dublin, his achievements were never forgotten in his native Cork. At no time was that more in evidence than on the occasion of his death in 1999. As the hearse carrying his remains passed through the city, Cork men and women lining the route burst into spontaneous applause. Exactly 60 years after the famous 'thunder and lightning' final, the people of Cork were still applauding one of the greatest sporting legends the county had ever produced.

2. JOHN KEANE

THERE WAS SOMETHING OF EPIC PROPORTIONS IN THE FINAL DAYS OF WATERFORD HURLER John Keane's life. In failing health, with circulation problems and sensing he was about to die, he embarked on a final odyssey to meet for one last time the great hurlers he had admired and respected. With the autumn of 1975 setting in, John travelled the roads of Leinster and Munster, first to Kilkenny, next to Cork, then to Kerry and onwards to Limerick to make final acquaintance with legendary friends and foes from the past.

John made it through three counties: Kilkenny, Cork and Kerry. Unfortunately, the journey was never completed. Like some wounded hero, the great John Keane died on the roadside without completing his mission. Aged 58, in October 1975 he passed away in County Limerick, bringing to a close the life and career of a legend who respectively played with and trained Waterford's historic All-Ireland winning teams of 1948 and '59, and who became one of hurling's most admired and respected exponents.

'His final illness was a hard illness,' Pat Fanning, former GAA President and friend, right-hand man and confidant of John Keane, recalls. 'He went through agony with his leg due to a heart condition. But he still suffered on and still worked on. He would be in the car with just a slipper on the foot. John, in his earlier days, could take a drink but such was his commitment to family and everything else that in 1943, after the county final, on a day when he was very badly injured, from that day until his final illness he never took a drink.

'In the final illness they decided he should take a whiskey and give up the cigarettes just to ease him and that's what he did. Amputation, if not recommended, was about to happen anyway. He told me himself that in no circumstances would he submit himself to amputation, that if he were to die he would die whole.

'But the most extraordinary thing of all, almost providential, as if some other influence or providence was at work, was that before he died he went to Kilkenny where he looked up the famous Jim Langton, who was one of his great rivals. They spent a couple of nights in Kilkenny talking about the long ago. He left Kilkenny, came home to Waterford and then he went on to Kinsale to meet with Jack Barrett, another old Cork hurler.

'From Barrett he went to Tralee where Jackie Power of Limerick was now living and working. He met with all of those. Then he was making his way to Limerick when he died on the side of the road. It was almost a pilgrimage, a premonition he had, and this was a pilgrimage before death. It was a most extraordinary thing. If you like, that was the man that was John Keane. I think it indicates the strength of character that was there. This was the man who, close to death, his only thing was to go around and visit those men with whom he shared so much of his life and so much of his skill.'

John Keane was, by all accounts, an extraordinary hurler. With a massive physique, he towered at the heart of defence bringing vision and leadership to the hurlers he played with. Friends, club-mates and opponents describe the sort of rare intelligence, skill and ability to take control that is only seen in great exponents of the game. As a centre-back he dominated play. Switched to centre-forward he could still determine the outcome of games, as he did later on in the famous 1948 All-Ireland final.

Born in Waterford in 1917, the story of John Keane's rise to hurling prominence began as a teenager in the grim 1930s. A naturally talented and skilful hurler, he played for Mount Sion as their dominance in Waterford hurling was about to begin. He became a central part in the club's many championship victories and in 1934 he helped bring All-Ireland junior honours to his native county. By the following year he was a regular in the senior side. By 1937, just into his twenties, the finished article was about to be revealed in a contest with fellow Munster contenders, Limerick.

There are many myths and legends concerning the early prowess of John Keane but few dispute his role in the extraordinary 1937 clash with Limerick. That powerful Limerick side had contested the previous four All-Ireland finals, winning two and narrowly missing out on three in a row due to a single-point loss to Kilkenny in 1935. At the core of Limerick senior hurling was the great Mick Mackey, who was producing for his county some of the finest skills ever seen on a hurling field. In the 1937 Munster championship, the Mick Mackey legend was about to be severely tested by a young hurler from Waterford by the name of John Keane.

'In 1937 he was only just out of his teens when he had that most extraordinary game against Mackey,' says Pat Fanning. 'Limerick were the great team of that era. They were the dominant force in hurling at that period and Mackey was at his zenith. I remember "Green Flag" writing in the *Irish Press* and describing them as one of the greatest combinations he had seen coming out of Munster in many a year. But Keane was magnificent in his youth, a magnificent figure of a man, strong, well-built, a head with fair hair set on his shoulders, a massive body and with plenty of speed. He outmatched Mackey that day. That was the beginning. It was that that bred the belief that they could come.'

In 1938, with John Keane a dominant force at the heart of defence, Waterford surprisingly cruised through the Munster semi-final by defeating Cork at Dungarvan. On a wet and windy day, players like Keane, John Fanning and Charlie Ware produced mighty performances, repelling wave after wave of Cork attacks. The final score of 5–2 to 1–3 far from flattered an extraordinary display by the Déise men against a Cork team tipped for great things in that year's championship.

The victory over Cork was followed by a Munster final triumph over Clare, which secured for Waterford their first-ever Munster senior hurling title. In the subsequent All-Ireland semi-final against Galway, Keane once again produced a massive performance. He dominated defence, played with style and produced an eye-catching 80-yard solo run past five defenders. Waterford's historic 1938 All-Ireland final appearance against Dublin was about to take place.

'In 1938, having beaten Clare in Cork in the Munster final, they hammered Galway and then went on to play Dublin in the All-Ireland final. In that All-Ireland, beaten by a couple of points, I must say that it was the occasion that caught hold of them. But even there, Keane was the dominant force at centre-back. He was a great man in 1938 and continued to be a great man until the end of his career,' according to Pat Fanning.

In the years following the All-Ireland defeat of 1938, Waterford's senior hurlers performed less than successfully in a long sequence of championship campaigns. Apart from losing bravely to Cork in a thrilling 1943 Munster final, the county seniors struggled to evolve into a team capable of winning provincial or All-Ireland titles. However, despite their failure to set the hurling world on fire, the team was slowly but surely maturing into a well-balanced, strong and skilful side. At the core of that team was John Keane; a player now recognised as a fearless, inspirational leader who led by his enormous skill and his courageous example.

'I recall 1943, against Tipperary, in Dungarvan,' says Pat Fanning. 'There was nobody closer than John Keane and myself, and I regard him as something of a hero figure, but this was a Cú Cualainn effort. His leg was so bad that none of us thought he could go out on the field. But he went out on the field and not only did he go out on the field that day against Tipperary but he played as if there was nothing wrong with him. His swollen ankle, his swollen foot, became more swollen as the game went on.

'After that game John was on the side of the field and he was sitting down on the line. He couldn't even go to the dressing-room. The leg was so swollen that I had to actually get a knife. We clipped off the laces and then clipped the boot open to ease it off his swollen foot. There was this man there, a horny old man of maybe 70 years of age at the time, and he came over. He was looking down at Keane and the leg and he said: "I'm happy now that I've seen John Keane hurl."'

As the 1940s progressed, a long-awaited All-Ireland triumph for Waterford seemed as elusive as ever. By 1948 talented players like Jim Ware, Andy Fleming, Mick Hickey (the captain in 1938) and Christy Moylan were in their thirties. Vin Baston, a tower of strength in midfield or defence, was, at 28, at the height of his hurling powers. The great John Keane, now aged 31 and 13 years on the road as a senior, had developed the sort of vision and command of a game required of legendary hurlers. For all these players, if it didn't happen soon it would never come at all.

In the 1948 championship campaign, Waterford beat Clare with John Keane playing at centre-forward and later in the game in defence. In the Munster final, the men from the Déise faced a Cork team containing players like Christy Ring, Jack Lynch and Willie John Daly. Without Phil Grimes, who had emigrated to America, Waterford were clearly the underdogs. However, on that fateful Sunday in August 1948, they defeated the Rebels by 4–7 to 3–9. Following a semi-final victory over Galway, where two goals were scored by Keane, a second historic appearance in an All-Ireland final now loomed.

'That was the greatest day in Waterford hurling,' Pat Fanning recalls. 'The era 1957–63 will probably be reckoned the greatest but to win your first All-Ireland and to couple that with the winning of the minor All-Ireland was a great achievement. In the lead up to it, training was done in Walsh Park in front of an attendance that would do justice to a county championship match. They were there night after night savouring every moment of it, drinking in the atmosphere, talking and arguing and wondering about what was to be. The days before that All-Ireland will never be forgotten.

'The team gathered in Waterford and left from Waterford. As the team left, the crowd cheered them on. All through that morning, all the buses and lorries and everything that was capable of moving were on the road. I don't think there was ever an exodus like it from any county, even though other counties have the population and we're a small county, relatively speaking. You often talk about pulling down the shutters after the last man has left. Certainly, in 1948 the number of people left in Waterford must have been very few. Our minors, incidentally, were based in Naas. The sight of Waterford people going through Naas and into Dublin was most extraordinary.'

From the throw-in at the 1948 All-Ireland final against Dublin, Waterford's resolute commitment was evident. Tight and determined in defence and sharp in attack, they burst into a lead of 1–2 to 0–0 after twenty minutes. In the twenty-third minute John Keane, playing at centre-forward, scored a goal that put the Déise men in command of the game. At half-time Waterford led by nine points. By full-time, powered by Vin Baston and John Keane, who had scored another goal, the lead had been stretched to an impressive 6–7 to 4–2. An elusive All-Ireland victory was secured for the first time in Waterford history.

Combined with the minors' All-Ireland success over Kilkenny earlier that day, Déise hurling had reached a pinnacle never witnessed before or since.

'John Keane played at centre-forward in 1948,' Pat Fanning says. 'In my mind now there's an image of him breaking through, beating a couple of men, the ball on his hurley. Then, unable to play the ball, he kicks it to the net. I can see him still, completely off the ground, both legs off the ground, meeting this ball and driving it into the net. But again, it was his influence over others that made the difference. He was the kingpin, although you had other great men like Vin Baston, God be good to him, Christy Moylan and all of those. But John stood out in the company of men; his sheer physical presence was almost overbearing. That was the day, I suppose, in which Waterford hurling came of age.

'I'm not exaggerating the situation when I say that in all of the critical games in which Waterford was engaged during his period and during my time, he was the man who made the difference. Even in defeat, he was a man who stood out, just as in 1937 the magnificence of him standing there at centre-back and throwing back the hordes of Limerick forwards that bore down on him. These are the pictures and images I have of John Keane. So it was in 1948, also, when he was gone past his zenith, I would say. He was on a down curve but he was still the great man. Of course, his hurling brain stood to him, he was the master of tactics and he was the natural leader of men who responded to his urgings.'

Andy Fleming, a colleague of John Keane on that victorious 1948 All-Ireland winning side, also remembers the great day. 'John Keane was fantastic,' he says. 'He was put up into centre-forward to strengthen the half-forward line. Vincent Baston took his position at centre-back. He dominated the whole half-forward line against Dublin. He organised all the moves. If he got the ball and couldn't hit it he'd distribute it. He'd pass it out for someone to run on to it. He was able to find loopholes in the Dublin back line. We beat them well that day.'

By all accounts, the return of the team to Waterford in 1948 was a truly remarkable occasion. The county's victorious minor and senior teams travelled together from Dublin and were eventually brought to a standstill at the outskirts of the city. There, surrounded by bonfires, the first of some 25,000 people crammed the roadsides. Press reports describe the colour of the occasion, the sound of boat and railway hooters, the music of local bands, the sea of blue and white cheering the teams to the City Hall for a civic reception. Never before had the city of Waterford seen anything like it.

'It was a reawakening in Waterford and everybody came out to greet us,' Andy Fleming recalls. 'We came home in cars and we were met about two or three miles out. We got up on the back of a big lorry and we came in through the town. You were only barely able to move across the bridge, down the quay and down to the mall. The lorry was only barely moving. People were trying to get up on deck with us and were trying to shake our hands. In fact, a young fellow was run over down at the bridge, crushed under the wheel and we didn't even know about it. We went and had a big "do" down at the Town Hall and up in De La Salle College we had a big dinner. It was unbelievable. Waterford hurling was dead up to then. But that started it off and it came on again up through the '50s.'

In the 1950s, having finally hung up his inter-county hurling boots, John Keane turned his attention to training the Waterford senior team. Under his guidance that team went on to unprecedented success, appearing in three All-Ireland finals and winning one. Playing fast and skilful hurling, Waterford narrowly lost the 1957 All-Ireland final to Kilkenny by a single point. They reversed their fortunes against Kilkenny in 1959 when, after a drawn first game, they won All-Ireland honours by a score of 3–12 to 1–10. They came close again in 1963 when losing a remarkable final to Kilkenny by 4–17 to 6–8. The inspirational skills of John Keane, once reserved for the playing fields, had steered a new era of Déise hurlers to national greatness.

'He was a very quiet, human individual,' Frankie Walsh, captain of Waterford's 1959 All-Ireland winning side recalls. 'He would not stand up in a dressing-room and make a big speech or anything. Pat Fanning did that for us. But the great thing about John was that if you did something on the field, and you weren't supposed to do it, afterwards he just called you aside and gave you a little talking to. I wouldn't say it was a talking to, as such. He'd tell you in a nice, polite way that you were a little bit better than that and you shouldn't do it again. That is the lovely thing I liked about John Keane: the human touch.'

'John had a hands-on approach to the training,' Austin Flynn, one of the backs on the team remembers. 'He was moving through the group the whole time with nine or ten hurling balls flying all over the place. He was stressing the whole time: "'Tis all in the wrist, lads, a flick of the wrist, that's all that's needed." John would be flicking the ball maybe ten feet away from you and you were constantly reaching further and further. The team was noted at the time for being exceptionally fast but I wasn't conscious that we were doing a pile of running. Really, the secret John had was that you were hunting a ball and clocking up the mileage in a very pleasant way.

'After the training we would be sitting down having the tea and sandwiches and John would sit in between you and the next fellow and he'd have a personal chat with you. He was drifting around. At the time you'd think he was only dealing with you but afterwards you saw that the other fellows were experiencing the same thing. He was a lovable character, very straight and very simple in his approach to life. I couldn't imagine John Keane having an enemy. Any time I met him I came away the better for it.'

'I never heard a word of criticism from him,' John Barron, another of the team's backs says. 'He never criticised the players. He never abused the players and said you were the cause of this score or that score. Instead, he'd come around and clap us on the back and say: "This is going to be a great game. You're going to win this and don't be nervous." He was a fatherly figure to us all and he'd put us at ease as well as he could.

'When I came on the Waterford team first, we were beaten in a league match by, I think, Kilkenny. I was in the dressing-room and John Keane came over to me and he said: "John," he said, speaking to me, "a little word of advice. When you make a mistake out there, don't let the whole place know you're after making a mistake. We all make mistakes, all the players do. But keep your mistakes to yourself." I probably had missed the ball and maybe thrown my hurley or made some gesture. But that was John Keane. He knew I had made a mistake but he didn't want me to tell the whole field that I had made a mistake.

'John knew it all. John was there before. When we went to the All-Ireland in 1957 we were edgy. Teams up for the first time are nervous. It's all new to them. Croke Park is new. The dressing-rooms are new.

Going up the night before, it's all strange. But we had John Keane. He was always one of the greats of Waterford hurling. For a man with such a record, we had not only a great regard for him as a hurler but also a great regard for him as a person.'

Throughout his career John Keane was inextricably linked with the great years of Déise hurling from 1938 to 1963. From Waterford's first Munster senior title and first All-Ireland appearance in 1938 through to their historic first All-Ireland success a decade later, his footsteps can be found along every step of the way.

A winner of seven Railway Cup medals, he also played with and captained his beloved Mount Sion to a seemingly endless succession of county championship victories. Then, to crown it all, he inspired his native county to their remarkable three All-Ireland appearances in the late 1950s and early '60s, winning a further All-Ireland along the way. Voted on to the Team of the Millennium, no other name comes close to matching his impact over a full quarter of a century of Waterford hurling history.

'After he died in 1975, Pat Fanning and myself went up to bring him back,' Frankie Walsh recalls. 'When we reached the bridge in Waterford, to see the crowd was unbelievable. The following day Pat Fanning gave an oration at the graveside and there were people from all over Munster and Leinster there. I think Pat's final farewell was: "You're a good one."

'Afterwards, Jackie Power of Limerick came up to the Mount Sion club. We had a few drinks and just before Jackie and his family left for Limerick he said he'd like to say a few words. He stood up and he said: "In my generation, John Keane taught the younger people how to hurl." I don't think you could pay any better tribute than what Jackie Power said that day.'

'I'll say this much,' Pat Fanning concludes, 'we produced many great men – Christy Moylan, Phil Grimes, Andy Fleming, Tom Cheasty, Charlie Ware – all of those in the early years. And people will often ask me: "Who was the best hurler Waterford ever produced?" I say: "If we're going to sit down and discuss it, we'll take John Keane out of it. Put John Keane to one side and then discuss the rest." I believe he was incomparable, the best hurler this county ever produced.

'I need only go to the evidence and the statements of other people in other counties to establish that he ranked with the highest in any era, and he was rated in an era of great hurlers. John Keane would stand in the best of company and would be there not merely on a level with them but superior to all but a very chosen few. I rank him with Ring, and his contribution to his club and to his county would not be surpassed by any other man's contribution to club or county.'

3. MICK MACKEY

SOMEWHERE BACK IN THE EARLY 1930S, MICK MACKEY PERFECTED THE ART OF THE SOLO run. Like all hurling inventions, it wasn't entirely new. In fact, it was Mick's father, the famous Limerick captain 'Tyler' Mackey, who is credited with first developing the technique. In the 1930s, however, Tyler's son combined speed, strength and dexterity with the art of balancing the ball on a hurley. With his eye on the goal, the ball on his stick and defenders collapsing around him, Mick Mackey's solo runs had a devastating impact on the sport of hurling in the 1930s and '40s.

Mackey's dazzling runs graced Munster finals and All-Ireland deciders at the height of Limerick's rise to hurling prominence. Hopping the ball on his stick, he launched 30- and 40-yard solo attacks in a succession of legendary contests. Charging for goal, brushing defenders aside, he stood out like a beacon at the height of his career. With four successive Munster championships from 1933 to 1936, two All-Irelands in 1934 and 1936 and further Munster and All-Ireland victories in 1940, few could match the achievements of the Ahane and Limerick hurler, Mick Mackey.

'Mick's hurling style wouldn't be something to be imitated because there was nobody who hurled like him,' Dr Dick Stokes, Mick Mackey's colleague in the 1940 All-Ireland winning Limerick team, declares. 'He had a unique method of hurling. He was a very strong, well-built man, very active. A lot of strong men can't use their strength. But Mick was very well put together and could use it. He could think, as well as everything else. He was a great traveller and a great runner. He mightn't be as good at hurling in the air as other fellows. But, my goodness, when it came down he could take it.

'He could throw fellows out of his way. He did it in a very purposeful way. In other words, it was not just loose strength or loose knocking of fellows about for the sake of knocking them about. It was always constructive. He made room for himself by his strength. When the fellows were knocked about, he was gone with the ball. He carried the ball. That was his method of doing it. He was unique, in that respect.

'He could go up through the middle, he never had to go up the sideline or anything like that. He had a great swerve. I can remember in my early days, when I saw him first, he'd be going out for a ball and he'd run against a fellow and the fellow was gone. Mick would be off with the ball. He had that knack. He had a great presence of things that were happening around him, as well. If, at any stage, someone was being beaten on the field, Mick was always able to handle that and solve it.

'You have fellows now carrying the ball and when some fellow catches him the ball is gone off his hurley. That didn't happen with Mick. He took it with him. He hurled short, if you like, putting the ball near him, and he was able to manoeuvre himself into a position that it just couldn't be taken off him. When he went with the solo runs he was a great man to finish them and score. He did an amount of scoring in every match he went into. He had a technique that was unique to him and nobody else that I ever saw. He was a match-winner on his own. He was a team by himself, really.'

If ever there was a person destined to hurl for his county, then Limerick's Mick Mackey certainly was that man. A native of the village of Castleconnell, he grew up in a family steeped in the traditions of the game. His grandfather, Michael Mackey, was a local hurler of some renown. Michael, in turn, was father to John 'Tyler' Mackey, who became one of the great legends of Limerick hurling in the early twentieth century. Tyler captained Limerick in the 1910 All-Ireland final. He established a reputation as a flamboyant, stylish player whose dashing runs and high-energy performances marked him out from his peers. He also practised those solo runs that his son would later make famous.

'Mick's grandfather was very much involved in the early days before the GAA was started,' Dick Stokes says. 'Two districts would beat a ball between them and have a match with no regulations. Whoever got it into their own district first won the match. Later, when the GAA was founded, the same man was very active in a very good Castleconnell team, the best in Limerick at the time. Mick's grandfather was captain of one of those teams. They were very famous.

'Michael Mackey had a son, known popularly as "Tyler". The name was due to a pair of boots that he bought in Limerick, in Tylers shop. He was pretty famous. He was captain of the Castleconnell team and he was a brilliant hurler. He played with Castleconnell from 1901 up to about 1917. He was known all over the country by friends and foes, and was very highly thought of.

'When we talk of Mick's prowess and what he's best known for, the solo run, it was his father who was an exponent of it. They were different characters. Apparently, Tyler was a fairly impetuous man in contrast to Mick, who was a very placid man. Mick did what he had to do on the field but outside of that he was a placid man. He wasn't an excitable man. There was a contrast in that respect.

'Tyler was a very strong character, a great leader, and was looked up to by his team and by others. People came to matches to see him play. Mick was also a strong character but in a different way. What he had to do he did without fear or favour but he wasn't an excitable fellow at all. He concentrated on his hurling and, if you like, other fellows were concentrating on him.'

In 1926 the newly formed Ahane GAA club caught the attention of a young Mick Mackey. At the time of the club's formation, Mick was fourteen. Within three years, he was winning his first medal with Ahane in the county junior hurling final. In time, he would win fifteen county senior hurling titles with Ahane. He also helped the club to victory in five county senior football finals.

Mick's brother John eventually followed in his big brother's footsteps and joined up with Ahane. Soon the two Mackeys were winning minor honours, securing winners' medals in the 1930 county minor final. The rise of the Mackeys was meteoric after that. In the early 1930s Mick played his first games for the county senior hurlers. In time, John followed suit and joined the county panel. The era of the Mackeys in Limerick's historic hurling side of the 1930s was about to begin.

'From 1933 on, the team built up,' Dick Stokes recalls. 'There was a nucleus there, mainly from Ahane. Good players came in. The whole lot of them were just phenomenal. You could hardly get a team to beat them, even though Kilkenny did it a couple of times. They were all great hurlers and they integrated terribly well. They were outstanding. It had built up to a phenomenal team by 1936, when they came to a peak.

'I can remember it as a young lad, growing up when Limerick were rising. The crossroads stuff at home, it was marvellous. There was a great atmosphere because they were winning all the time. Every young fellow was hurling because of the team. It really was a great era to be living in, from that point of view. It did a lot for the country, as well. Things weren't always that great in those days. That gave things a lift in local areas.

'The radio was only coming in. It was sparse enough. Only certain houses had radios, where we all congregated. The radio was put out on the sill of the window. There was another thing that used to happen in those early days in Thurles. I think it was a Cork phenomenon. When the match was over, pigeons were released. I have never seen this written up anywhere. There were carrier pigeons released on the pitch when the match was over, to bring the news of who won back to Cork.'

The remarkable rise of Limerick in the 1930s began in Munster in1933. Following a pitch invasion, Limerick, who were leading 3–7 to 1–2, were awarded the Munster crown. Already, players like the great goalkeeper Paddy Scanlan, Timmy Ryan, along with Mick and John Mackey, were showing exceptional skill. Having emerged from Munster, they powered their way to the 1933 All-Ireland final, where they lost to Kilkenny. In 1934, however, they returned to Croke Park where they beat Dublin in a replay to win the side's first All-Ireland title.

A succession of great Munster contests followed. Starting in 1933, Limerick won four Munster finals in succession, defeating all the great Munster powers along the way. They once more lost to Kilkenny in the 1935 All-Ireland final but they learned from their mistakes and they were back the following year to win another historic All-Ireland title. That year, 1936, marked the peak for Limerick, partly because of the quality of players who had blossomed and partly because they gained revenge over old enemies, Kilkenny. Add on the no little matter of five National Hurling League titles in succession, from 1934 to 1938, and you get some idea of the power of the Limerick side of the 1930s.

'They had a unique bunch of fellows together at that time,' Dick Stokes says. 'Fellows looked after their own corner, their own part of the field, their own man on the field. That was traditional, that was the way it was done. But Mick, on his own, when he got the ball in his heyday, he was able to take it on his own. He wasn't selfish or unique in that respect. They were all very good hurlers. But Mick could take it on his own. He didn't need anybody.

'He reached his peak, I'd say, in '36, the same as the rest. He was a tower of strength. He was the leading figure in the whole thing, outside of the scores he got, which were many. The whole thing was built around him. The others were all very good. But he was super and if there was a score wanted he got it.'

It took until the early 1940s for the paths of hurling's two greatest exponents, Mick Mackey and Christy Ring, to face each other on the field of play. Conventional wisdom pinpoints the sheer physical strength of Mackey compared to the style and the class of Ring. Observers who knew both highlight Mackey's laid-back, cool demeanour in contrast to Ring's awesome intensity. Both scored extraordinary goals from solo runs, although Mackey made the practice a central feature of his game while Ring excelled at air and ground hurling. Ultimately, while both clearly were exceptionally talented, Ring was obsessive while Mackey took it more in his stride.

'You couldn't compare them,' Dick Stokes says. 'I believe they played on one another and they said it was 50-50. I don't know if that's true or not. They were two different types of hurlers completely. Christy was very sharp, accurate, tense, I might say. He was a great hurler, no question about it, and a match-winner in many instances. I played in Railway Cups which he was the winner of, in a number of cases, with snap scores and so on. Mick was more even as a person, he didn't get too excited about it before or after. He was a different kind of character. You couldn't compare the two of them at all. They were completely different, maybe equally effective but with different styles.'

What is clear is the extraordinary psychology used by both players in the course of a game. Ring was obsessed with referees, constantly evaluating their characteristics and weaknesses. He also pressed players with other counties, particularly those he partnered on Munster Railway Cup sides, for information about future opponents.

Mackey, on the other hand, wasn't afraid to press home his physical advantage in the course of a game. With a smile on his face, as Jack Lynch said, he'd 'hit you hard'. Described as a 'rogue' by many who knew him, putting opponents in their place wasn't unknown to Mick Mackey.

'I don't mean it in any derogatory way but Mick was a trickster on the field,' Dick Stokes remarks. 'He played the scene he was in and he played the fellow as well. He analysed the fellows he was playing on and he knew how to handle them. He was able to use different methods to deal with different people. He would play the fellow he was on psychologically. He had the aptitude to do that.

'With some particular individual, he might use his strength and his agility. He was able to use that strength to great effect, to put fellows off a bit, to shake them up a bit. He used that where it was necessary and was very well able to do it. He had that presence, he understood where he was on the field and he understood all the psychology of the thing, without turning it into a profession.'

In the latter years of the 1930s Limerick's fortunes dipped somewhat, with the county losing out to Tipperary (1937) and Cork (1939) in tight, hard-fought Munster finals. There were, however, National Hurling League victories in 1937 and 1938. There also were many superb hurling confrontations, especially in 1939 when Cork and Limerick served up one of the finest classics in Munster hurling history. That year, Cork won. Things would change in 1940.

In September 1940 Mick Mackey captained Limerick to victory for the second time in an All-Ireland final. Having already captained the side to success in 1936, he led Limerick in the 1940 decider against Kilkenny. His side had earlier beaten Cork in a dramatic and memorable Munster final, which went to a replay. Old hands like Paddy Scanlan, Jackie Power, Timmy Ryan, John Mackey, Paddy McMahon and Paddy Clohessy formed the backbone of that team. New recruits included Dick Stokes who, in his first senior inter-county year, won a coveted All-Ireland medal.

'In 1940 we were two points behind at half-time against Kilkenny,' Dick recalls. 'Positional changes were made, the principal one being that Mick went out centre-field with Timmy Ryan and scored two points from outside. Then we got a goal. The whole thing began to come. Limerick just started moving. Sorry, Mick started moving. He went out at centre-field, he'd go anywhere, he'd go back to the backs or go into the forwards, wherever there was something to be done.

'It was great, I suppose. We didn't appreciate what it meant. I remember resting with Paddy McMahon before we went out to play the 1940 final. Paddy had been in two or three of them and he appreciated it. I was a young fellow. I didn't appreciate it as much as I should. But it was a great era.'

Limerick's prominence lasted throughout the war years and beyond, with many legendary battles fought against Cork. Unfortunately, the war years brought tragedy to the Mackey family. In early 1941 a third brother, Paddy Mackey, died and both Mick and John withdrew for the rest of that year's hurling campaign as a mark of respect. The war years also saw Mick join the army, where he kept in shape by playing with his fellow-soldiers. Playing at both brigade and divisional levels, he turned in some exemplary performances while adding to his medal collection.

These were the 'Emergency' years, with rationing, blackouts and a shortage of fuel for all modes of transport. With trains restricted and cars unable to travel, getting to matches became a difficult chore. Roads were crammed with supporters travelling by bicycle to Munster finals and All-Ireland deciders. They cycled from Dublin to Thurles and they travelled by bicycle from all over Munster to see the great battles between Mick Mackey of Limerick and Christy Ring and Jack Lynch of Cork.

'The bicycle era happened because cars weren't allowed to go to matches,' Dick says. 'In some areas, funerals were set up to follow a coffin but, generally speaking, fellows set off on their bicycles, maybe with hay in the tyre instead of a tube. Some would even have walked or got lifts in long-cars or pony and traps. All sorts of things hit Thurles at that time.

'The 1944 Munster final was a famous one and Limerick and Cork played the usual draw in a most exciting match. The replay of that was the same type again, hell for leather. It ended up where Mick went in with a ball and scored a goal. But there was a free and the free was given instead of the goal. The free was missed. Cork won by three points, so it wasn't too bad for the taker.

'That was a most exciting match, with the same tempo as the other matches between Cork and Limerick. It was the end of an era, in a way. Cork and Limerick played again in 1946 and Mick was playing corner-forward this time. But he was still playing and still getting scores. He had a long spell. Ring maybe lasted longer; he was a different type of hurler. But Mick was very effective up to when he finished in 1946. That was the end of him.'

Following the 1946 Munster final, Mick Mackey effectively retired from inter-county hurling. He stayed on at club level with Ahane, where he added to his county hurling championship haul, bringing the total to 15. He also won a career total of five county football championships with his club. Despite Mick's retirement, his brother John played at the highest level for a few more years, continuing to perform with distinction for Limerick. Beside him, Mick engrossed himself in other facets of hurling, officiating at games, training the Limerick team in the 1950s and bringing his experience and knowledge of the game to the Munster team.

Like most great hurlers, playing in great teams, Mick Mackey left the game with a healthy haul of silverware. To his three All-Ireland senior hurling medals he added five National Hurling Leagues and five Munster championships. There were also eight Railway Cup medals won with a star-studded Munster side. But it wasn't for the trophies that Mick Mackey is remembered. Instead, the image remains of a dark, strong, handsome hurler terrorising defences, controlling games and scoring vital goals and points. Sometimes he did it in his socks. Other times he did it with such effect that he chalked up tallies like the 5–3 he scored in the 1936 Munster final. Either way, his name is recalled, along with Ring, as one of the greatest hurlers the game has ever produced.

Perhaps it was inevitable that, following his death in September 1982, one of the largest-ever funerals took place in County Limerick. They travelled from all over Munster and beyond to pay one last tribute to Limerick's famous son. From the removal in Limerick to the burial in Castleconnell, crowds thronged the route. Accompanied by an honour guard of former team-mates from Ahane and Limerick, Mick Mackey's remains were laid to rest in Castleconnell where, all those years before, in the early 1930s, Limerick's greatest-ever hurling odyssey first began.

'Friends and foes respected him and they all turned up in Castleconnell,' Dick Stokes, who remained in top-class hurling into the 1950s, concludes. 'His funeral was the biggest ever seen in Castleconnell. The amount of compliments that were paid afterwards by people was phenomenal. He was a unique character in hurling in the country, not just in Limerick, and that was reflected in the attitude towards him when he was dead. It was colossal the compliments paid by all the fellows who played against him and with him, but especially by the fellows who played against him. They all respected him highly.

'I'd rate Mick tops, not because he's a Limerick man. We heard of these miracle men in other places but Mick in my book was way ahead. He had all these assets; what he was as a man, his attitude towards the whole thing, his ability, the length of time he was at it, the things that he achieved. They were all out of the top drawer. He was unique, in that way.

'We didn't appreciate it at the time. To be involved with a team like that and to be involved with the likes of Mick Mackey was something that fellows would have given their two eyes for. We took it in our stride. We were country lads and we looked on it as a normal kind of situation. I'm a fellow who takes things in a very normal way, I hope. But when you look back on it, I suppose, you can appreciate it more than you could at the time. It was a great era.'

4. CHRISTY RING

ON A BITTERLY COLD DAY IN THE LATE 1950S THE CREAM OF MUNSTER HURLERS converged on Galway for a Railway Cup match. Those were the days when huge crowds flocked to Railway Cup contests. They were drawn by the style and power of the Cork and Tipperary players not to mention the speed and skill of the Waterford stars who, at the time, were making their mark on the game. Above all, they arrived to witness the genius of Cork's Christy Ring.

That day, Waterford's Phil Grimes, Séamus Power and John Barron were among the first to arrive. Tired from the journey and bitterly cold, they adjourned to a local hotel for some pre-match food. Soon, the Cork contingent caught up with the men from the Déise. This being Lent, some hard choices had to be made. Ravaged by hunger, the Waterford players reached a simple decision. For the Cork hurlers, led by Ring, the choice was far more austere.

'It was a beautiful hotel,' Waterford's John Barron recalls. 'Steak and chips was the dominant order on the menu. It was Lent and we weren't allowed to eat meat. However, we argued that we were travellers and we went for the steak and chips. We did the correct thing, if memory serves me right. It was a beautiful meal.

'During the meal who came in only Christy Ring, Jimmy Brohan, Paddy Barry and one or two other Cork players. I think it was a party of five. They sat down at the table beside us and speculation started about what they were going to eat. But when the waitress came over to the table Ring stood up and said: "Boiled eggs for everyone." He said: "Boiled eggs and that's that." There was no dissenting voice, even though there was a beautiful odour of steak and chips. All the Cork players settled for boiled eggs.

'He was supremely confident. In particular, he was supremely confident of his own ability. I remember listening to a discussion between himself and, I think, Phil Grimes, Séamus Power and Martin Óg Morrissey before a Railway Cup final on St Patrick's Day. It was a big thing in those days. To listen to Christy, there was only one hurler – and that was Christy Ring.

'Even his team-mates he had no great regard for, not even the best of Cork hurlers, which really surprised me. But that was Christy Ring. Anyone who knew him knew that his team-mates idolised him. But I suppose he believed that other players would never come up to his standard. And he was right, of course.'

Arguably no other player in the history of hurling could match the skill and personal magnetism of Cork's Christy Ring. Revered by fellow players and feared by opponents, he left an indelible mark on all he encountered in his long hurling career. From his days as a minor in the late 1930s to his retirement in the 1960s, Christy captivated crowds like no player before or since.

It was said, at the time, that Christy's name on the team-sheet guaranteed an extra 10,000 or 20,000 on the gate. Railway Cup matches offered hurling supporters from as far away as Connacht and Ulster the rare chance to witness his skills. Spectators with only a passing interest in hurling travelled to Croke Park to see him play in Railway Cup finals on St Patrick's Day.

Fortunately his appearances were many, resulting in an astonishing record of 18 Railway Cup medals won with Munster between 1942 and 1963, to add to his record eight senior All-Ireland medals won with Cork. His career also spanned the generations, encompassing Cork's famous wartime four-in-a-row, the titanic All-Ireland battles with Wexford in the 1950s, right through to his latter years during Ireland's economic boom in the early 1960s.

'I remember him from when I was a child,' recalls Tipperary legend Jimmy Doyle, who idolised Ring in the late 1940s. 'Tipperary would play Cork in Thurles and I'd follow them down to the Glenmorgan House. I suppose I was eight or nine. I used to make my way to the Glenmorgan and watch Christy eating his dinner. I was so excited, I wanted to see what he ate.

'He had a big pair of wrists on him, he was a powerful man. He'd eat his dinner and then, when he was finished, he'd walk out. I'd be so small I'd be hiding behind a partition. I'd follow him down the Square and back up the other side. I used to follow him all over the town. I'd follow every move he made. I adored him, I thought he was absolutely brilliant.

'Later on, when I played with and against him, I'd stand and watch him and look at him. I'd fool around like he did. I'd see him tipping a ball before the game, hitting it into the air and controlling it on his hurley before it hit the ground. I used to do that. I'd hit the ball upfield and, as it was dropping, I'd run on to it and control it. When I started, I found it very hard to do. But eventually I was able to get it on to the hurley and hold it and control it.

'He could make a ball talk. He was so brilliant you always had to keep an eye on him. And he practised a lot. I remember one Railway Cup match, we were up in Barry's Hotel in Dublin and I was sharing the room with him. I slept in the bed beside him. He was in one bed and I was in the other. He got out his hurley and a ball from the bag and he started banging the ball from one wall to the other. He was snapping it and hitting it and the ball was flying over my face. I said to him: "Christy, what are you doing at all?" He said: "I'm trying to keep my eye in."

'Another time, we were playing Ulster in Belfast and we were going up on the train. We pulled in to Belfast and he got out of the train and he put on his cap. I said: "Christy, why are you putting the cap on?" "Ah, well," he said, "I don't want to be recognised." But you'd always recognise Christy. You'd know him anywhere because he was such a brilliant player.'

The rise of Christy Ring began at a time when the dark shadows of war hung over Europe. Already victorious as a Cork minor, Christy soon progressed to a Cork senior side that would sweep all before it during the grim war years. His major début, at the age of 19, was in a victorious league match against Kilkenny in October 1939.

In his early years with the seniors Christy was overshadowed, perhaps even overawed, by the talent at Cork's disposal. Cork's star-studded side was crammed with players of the calibre of Jack Lynch, John Quirke, Con Murphy, Seán Condon and Mick Kenefick. In such elevated company, it took Christy time to adjust to the big stage.

In less than half a decade, however, as the nation came to terms with rationing and wartime austerity, Cork and the young Christy Ring powered their way to unprecedented hurling success. Three All-Ireland victories over Dublin and a further victory over Antrim guaranteed for that great team their place in history as winners of a unique four-in-a-row. Those victories from 1941 to 1944 also secured for Christy his first four senior All-Ireland medals.

'I was always taken aback by his vision of the game,' says Con Murphy, who played alongside Christy in three of Cork's four-in-a-row victories. 'He had great anticipation, a great sense of where the ball was going to be. He also had the presence to take the short-cut to get somewhere when others would be floundering, wondering what was going to happen next. He was able to read the game perfectly. He had a wider range of skills than any other player that I ever saw.

'He developed his skills by practising by himself, devoting time and hours of concentration. As a tanker driver for Irish Shell, he used to carry the hurley in the cab and call in to different fields. I know one of them where, on a regular basis, he used to go with his hurley. He had a target some bit away from him and he'd practise frees and pick spots for scoring.

'He was very accurate. His strokes were like bullets when he hit the ball. And he developed the 21-yard free-taking style that we see other people using now. He would lift and then move the ball in a bit before getting the full power behind it. It's a very skilful thing to do, to be able to synchronise your movement and strike the ball maybe a yard further in than where you were standing when you lifted it. He succeeded in perfecting that and he got goal after goal by using it.'

There are many moments of hurling brilliance that stand out in the long career of the great Christy Ring. All-Ireland final day in September 1946, when Christy won his fifth All-Ireland medal, is remembered for one of those moments. As captain of Cork, Christy soloed the ball a full 70 yards, hopping the sliotar off his hurley, easing his way past the Kilkenny defenders and flicking the ball to the back of the net.

Two years before, in the 1944 Munster final, he had also shown exceptional flair, this time in the closing minute against Mick Mackey's Limerick. Once again, Ring soloed the ball from the half-back line and sent a 40-yard rocket to the back of the net. That day, Cork squeezed past Limerick by 4–6 to 3–6, winning the Munster final, and the growing legend of Christy Ring was further enhanced.

Throughout those years in the mid-1940s Christy flourished in his new role as Cork's inspiration and driving force. He chalked up a succession of Munster championships with Cork and a further succession of club championships with Glen Rovers. He also immersed himself in hurling, studying the game, obsessively practising, scrutinising fellow players, relentlessly analysing performances and carrying an intensity and passion on to the field that has never been witnessed before or since in the sport of hurling.

'He was fanatical,' says Wexford's Billy Rackard. 'I remember I played on the Rest of Ireland team with him once. That was a tea-party affair, no one took it seriously. But I watched him in the dressing-room and he was so uptight. He had all the symptoms that you notice when a player is uptight: he's testing his hurley stick, he's re-tightening his shoes, he's going in and out of the toilet, absolutely coiled up.

'I remember a lad ran over looking for his autograph but he was so focused he just wouldn't do it, he moved on. All that energy had to be released, he was a great man to focus his energy in the right direction. He was a pretty tough man, he'd be merciless if you were acting up on him. If he thought you weren't behaving yourself, he'd quickly let you know, verbally and physically. He had a woeful strong stroke on a ball and he'd fairly well wrap that stick around you.'

'I'm inclined to say it was a kind of hurling madness,' says Clare's Jimmy Smyth. 'Even though he was fairly lucid while he was playing, yet he had this kind of hurling madness that brought him out of the ordinary hurler's sphere. The minute he came on to a pitch anywhere, every daisy on it got a very, very fast death. He was pulling on the daisies and he was very, very strong. That's what he said himself, that he never met a man stronger than himself. I would believe that.'

'He split me across the ear once,' recalls Waterford's Andy Fleming. 'It was a league match between Waterford and Cork, up in Dungarvan. I played centre-back and Christy Ring was centre-forward for Cork. I was playing on Christy. Things went very bad for Christy. I was hurling Christy upside down. Then, in the last quarter of an hour, there was a high ball coming in. He split me across the ear.

'I was down on the ground and blood was splattering all over the place. When I was down, and the fellows were putting the bandage on, Christy ran over to me. He looked down at me. "Ah, Andy," he said. "I'm sorry I didn't do that to you an hour ago." Now, we were friends at the time. But he said: "I should have done that to you an hour ago, at the beginning of the game, not at the end of it."

'That scar there on my jaw is from Christy Ring,' says Tipperary's John Doyle. 'There was a shemozzle down in Cork and I wasn't involved in it. It was between a Tipperary man and Ring. They had a bit of a tussle. I don't know what happened but I was down on the ground anyway and when I got up Ring gave me an old flick of the hurley and got me there on the chin. I had to get four stitches on my chin. He'd take no prisoners. He was a fierce man, he contested everything.

'He was an unusual guy because he was his own man. I had one great experience with him when I went for the Senate back in the late '60s. I was down in Cork doing a bit of canvassing. I drove into Johnny Quirke's pub in Cork and when I went in who was inside only the bold Christy himself. Christy said to me: "What are you doing down here?" I explained to him what I was doing. He said: "I'll go with you." I nearly dropped. Christy got in the car with me and we spent the whole day going around Cork canvassing for the Senate for me. I couldn't believe it but it's true.'

'I suppose it was his enthusiasm for the game that gave people the impression that he was a fanatic,' Con Murphy, who later became a prominent Cork administrator, says. 'But he was a gentleman at heart and a man full of compassion. I hate to think that we were on strained relations at one time over stand tickets. I was Secretary of the County Board and I didn't give him enough stand tickets. He fell out very badly with me. He took a very poor view of my being stingy, as he said, with the stand tickets.

'I tried to explain to him that I had to be stingy because any one person couldn't get the lot. But I didn't win, anyway, and we went different ways. Eventually, I happened to be rushed into hospital and the first man in to see me was Christy, to know how I was. This is evidence, I think, of the humanity in the man and the compassion he had for everybody. He showed that in more ways than one over the years. From there on in, we were the best of friends.'

'Well, I travelled to America with Christy Ring in 1966,' Waterford's Austin Flynn says, recalling the humorous and obsessive sides of Ring. 'I got to know him fairly well at that stage. He told me that the first time he went hurling to America, Jim Barry went with him. They were coming out from Gaelic Park one day, which was a big distance from Manhattan. Barry called him over to a shop and said: "Look, that's a lovely dinner set. Buy it and bring it home to your sister." Christy wasn't married at the time. Christy bought the box anyway and Barry bought another box. Then Christy forgot all about it. But the day he was about to leave, he was in hiding in the hotel because everybody wanted to bring him out to their place. He went for a lie-down in the bed and he was looking at the box. He picked up the box and he opened it. There wasn't a good cup in it. They were all broken. He insisted that "There's no so-and-so going to cod us Cork fellas." So he went back up there looking for this shop again. He found the shop and he gave hell to the shopkeeper. The fellow had to count out each cup and pack it in front of him. He wasted a whole day doing that.'

In the 1950s Christy Ring reached further heights, winning another three senior All-Ireland medals during Cork's three-in-a-row from 1952 to 1954. He delivered many legendary performances in that decade, among them securing the 1954 Munster final for Cork by setting up a match-winning goal in lost time. He also scored three extraordinary match-winning goals in the final minutes of the 1956 Munster final against Limerick. He was deprived of a ninth All-Ireland medal only by the heroics of Wexford goalkeeper, Art Foley, in the 1956 All-Ireland final.

'You would hear people saying about the fluky goal that Ring got,' says Waterford's Austin Flynn. 'But from the time he went out on the field, he never took his eyes off the ball. The fluky goal that Ring got was the ball that everybody else was assuming was going to go over the bar or go wide. But Ring kept on running in case it hit off somebody or fell down and he'd score a goal.'

'It was quite an experience to play on him,' says Wexford's Billy Rackard, who marked Christy and who once held him scoreless. 'He had this ability, which a lot of present-day forwards haven't got, to pull first-time, in the most awkward positions, maybe with his back to the goal and he racing onto the ball.

'He was like a ballet dancer, he'd just pull and turn in the one movement and maybe score a point. Another player would have to stop it, work it around, to get in a proper shot. He was incredibly balanced. It has always been a theory of mine that Ring stayed in the game longer because he escaped a lot of would-be tackles by virtue of his first-time shooting.'

'Ring bought a car in 1952,' recalls Willie John Daly, an outstanding hurler who shared Cork's success with Christy in the 1950s. 'I remember the number of it well. It was ZD 6001. Ring drove it, of course. We'd have six in the car. I'd sit beside him in front. Jim Barry, Tony O'Shaughnessy and Mattie Fouhy would be there as well. And then, on other occasions, there would be Pat Barry.

'It was a misfortune to be sitting beside Ring in the front. Ring and Jim Barry would sometimes be arguing all the way home, maybe about the match. Ring would hit me on the arm when he'd be making a point against Jim Barry. I'd be sore for a couple of days afterwards in the arm because of the strength of him.

'He was a grand singer. Himself and Jim Barry would sing on the way home. He was great company and he was very witty. He could go back a long way on Irish history. He was a brilliant, very intelligent man but then a shy man as well. He had no hesitation in giving an autograph to a lad who'd have an autograph book but he would resent very much a young fellow who'd come over with a cigarette box. He had all these mannerisms but we loved him and we enjoyed him. He was a great friend to have.

'Somehow, he was always brilliant in the Railway Cup. People would come down from Belfast and they'd tell you: "We're coming down specially to see Christy Ring." The crowds enjoyed watching him play. He was always giving it his best. Mattie Fouhy and myself happened to be playing with him in the Railway Cup in 1954. The attendance that day was over 49,000. When Christy retired, after about five or six years, the attendance was down to 600.

'He had everything. I never saw Christy Ring missing a ball off the air or when going first-time at it on the ground, no matter what way it came, left or right. He was accurate every way and he won games that seemed to be lost. He was well marked, as the fella says, but at the same time Ring got the goals that counted.'

By the late 1950s Christy Ring was heading towards 40 and the Cork senior team was in transition. Willie John Daly, Mattie Fouhy, Josie Hartnett, Tony O'Shaughnessy and Gerald Murphy had left. Following a hugely successful decade, with four Munster championships and three All-Irelands, the impetus was gone from the Rebels who were now surpassed in Munster by neighbours Tipperary and Waterford.

That fallow period in the late 1950s also brought to public attention perhaps the greatest mystery of Christy Ring's career, involving an altercation between himself and Mick Mackey during the 1957 Munster semi-final between Cork and Tipperary. The incident, recorded in a remarkable photograph, clearly shows an injured Ring walking from the field of play while coldly trading remarks with Mackey, who was dressed in an umpire's white coat.

Coming in the wake of a controversial 'goal', where the Cork goalkeeper was charged to the net by two Tipperary forwards, the acidic tone of the picture tells its own tale. As it happened, the umpire Mackey had allowed the 'goal', only to be overruled by the referee. Up to their deaths, both Mackey and Ring steadfastly refused to reveal the details of their conversation – a contemptuous if fairly innocuous one, it now transpires.

'One of the umpires that day was Mick Mackey and the other umpire was a De La Salle colleague of mine, the late Dick Dalton,' Waterford's John Barron reveals. 'Dick had the point flag and Mick Mackey had the green flag. In goal for Cork that day was Mick Cashman.

'A high ball came in at Dick Dalton's point side of the goal. There were two or three forwards coming in with it. Mick Cashman knew that if he caught the ball, then the ball and Mick were in the back of the net. He palmed the ball out for a seventy. It all happened in a split second and Mick Cashman and two of the Tipperary forwards were in the back of the net. But the ball was over the end line.

'Mick Mackey hadn't the full view of what happened on the far side. He assumed the ball was in the back of the net and he immediately raised the green flag. My colleague, Dick Dalton, had his hand up for a seventy. There was great competition between Cork and Tipperary at that time and the place was bedlam. Christy Ring was corner-forward at the other end and raced up the field. Mackey jumped into the back of the net, picked up one of the spare hurleys and confronted Ring. The referee came in and cleared it up. It was a definite seventy. Mick was in the wrong, just a mistake.

'Later on in the game, Christy Ring took a tumble. He broke his wrist in that tumble, a quite simple fall, and he left the field of play. When he was bandaged up, he left the sideline and went to cross over to his own team-mates on the far side. He crossed behind Mick Mackey's goal where the confrontation had taken place.

'There's a lot of speculation about the language, or bad language, that passed between Mick and Christy Ring. However, my team-mate Dick Dalton said that what Christy Ring said to Mick Mackey was "Well, Mick, you never lost it." Mackey turned around and he said: "And neither did you, Christy." There was no abusive language or bad language or anything like that. That's the story I heard from Dick Dalton.'

In 1964, approaching the age of 44, Christy Ring was finally dropped from the Cork senior panel. In the following years, however, he continued to play for Glen Rovers, winning his thirteenth and fourteenth county club medals in 1964 and 1967 respectively. These he added to his eight All-Irelands, 18 Railway Cups, nine Munster Championships, four National Hurling Leagues and his single club senior football medal won in 1954.

In the following years, Christy Ring became a Cork county hurling selector. He also turned his attention to squash, which he played with the same determination and skill he once displayed at hurling. Then, in March 1979, Christy unexpectedly died, having collapsed near Cork's School of Commerce at the age of 58, thus bringing to a close the life and career of Cloyne's most famous son – the great Hall of Fame, Team of the Century and Team of the Millennium legend, Christy Ring.

'There will never again be a Christy Ring, in my opinion,' says Con Murphy. 'It would be great if there were. But changes have taken place since his time and I wonder how he'd fit in to being told what to do on the field, how to fit into a plan. Christy never operated to a plan, he couldn't.

'But there is no doubt about it that he was the greatest of them all.

He had the greatest range of skills. He thought the game through so correctly. He devoted so much of his time and energy to developing himself as a player and encouraging his team-mates. I wish there were more coming along like him. But I don't ever see him being equalled in the hurling arena again.'

5. TONY REDDIN

MAYHEM AND MADNESS PREVAILED AT THE MUNSTER HURLING FINAL IN KILLARNEY IN 1950. The official attendance that day was just under 39,000, although an estimated 10,000 to 15,000 more got in without paying. That was the day the crowd climbed walls and broke down gates to witness the great event. It was also the day when Tipperary legend and future goalkeeper on the Team of the Millennium, Tony Reddin, feared for his physical safety.

For Tipperary, it was indeed a battle royal as they sought a second Munster title in succession at the expense of bitter enemies, Cork. Tipperary surged into a seemingly unassailable lead. As the Rebels hauled themselves back into the game, the mood turned nasty. Christy Ring scored an inevitable goal. The swollen crowd spilled on to the field. Hundreds of Cork supporters congregated at the Tipperary end.

In the chaos that followed, they jostled and harassed the goalkeeper, hurled abuse, impeded his puck-outs and tore down the net. Even appeals from Cork's Jack Lynch couldn't calm the frenzied supporters. By the end of the game, tensions were so high that the goalkeeper had to be smuggled from the pitch in disguise. Tipperary had won what, by all accounts, was one of the most frenetic finals in the history of Munster hurling.

'I played very well in the first half,' Tony Reddin recalls. 'There was no crowd behind my back at the time. At half-time I could see all the Cork crowd going down to the bottom of the goal. The Tipperary backs said: "God, Reddin, you'd better mind yourself down there." I said: "I'm all right." I hurled hard, anyway, and I blocked every one of the balls and cleared them down every time. The crowd was on top of me in the second half and I'm in the middle. With ten minutes left to go I stopped the ball and this blackcoat [Galway expression for a supporter] fired a topcoat in my face. I cleared the ball and I had to pick up the topcoat and bring it back to the net.

'Another shot came in then. I blocked it again, caught it and they fired a cap in my face. But I cleared the ball again. They were throwing stuff on top of my head. I saw Jack Lynch walk over to keep the crowd back. I think Jack Lynch got a belt too as he tried to keep the crowd back. He couldn't do anything; he couldn't keep them back. I couldn't look back because I was afraid I would get a belt in the face. But I looked back with about three minutes to go and wasn't the back of the net gone!

'The very minute the match was over I walked out a bit and the Cork forwards and the Tipperary backs ran down and saved me. A priest gave me a hat. A blackcoat gave me a short coat and the priest took the hurley off me and gave it to the County Board. I had to stay on the pitch for two hours. All the Tipperary team had got in the cars and some of the lads shouted: "Where are you going? Bloody old Reddin is still on the pitch." They had 20 around me. I wanted to go but they wouldn't let me go. They said I had to wait for a while. I was late for the dinner. Tipperary stayed below on the road while I ate upstairs by myself. We couldn't put up the cup in the car. We had to go out to the Cork road, pull up and put up the cup and put up the flag all the way home to Thurles.'

That day in Killarney in 1950 marked the beginning of one of the finest and most competitive eras in the history of Munster hurling. In the years ahead, there would be equally intense battles between Cork and Tipperary. In fact, in five straight finals from 1950 to 1954 the two counties met time and again as they battled for the provincial crown. For the victors, it was a case of 'winner takes all'. In 1950 and '51 Tipperary emerged from Munster to become All-Ireland champions. The following years, 1952 to 1954, Cork went to Croke Park to win a famous three-in-a-row.

It says something about Cork and Tipperary hurling that four legends from the Team of the Millennium played in that first tumultuous final in Killarney. For Cork's Jack Lynch it marked the end of a distinguished career; for Christy Ring there would be another decade and more of greatness. For Tipperary's John Doyle it was the early days of a hurling odyssey that, in time, would secure a joint record with Ring of eight All-Ireland medals. For Tony Reddin, that Munster final was just part of a run of Munster and All-Ireland success that would help establish him as the finest goalkeeper in hurling history.

Ironically, the story of Tony Reddin began not in Tipperary but in County Galway, where he was born in 1919. He grew up in Mullagh, where he first began hurling on the family farm and eventually progressed to the county junior and senior teams. 'We had too much to do at home in Galway,' Tony says. 'I had to plough with a horse in those days. I'd hold the plough and I'd have a ball in my pocket. There were two wheels to the plough and a very long field. I'd let the horse pull away and I'd keep practising up and down with the hurley in my hand. Then I'd come out from the dinner and stay practising against the wall until I'd go down the field to plough it again. I ploughed every day and I hurled every day.

'In 1933 I played in the county final for Mullagh. I played centre-field in the first county final we ever won. I was picked for the minors and wasn't good enough for that. Then I was on the Galway juniors in 1940. We got into the All-Ireland final against Cork but we didn't do any good. Then I was on the Galway seniors and we didn't do any good. I also played in the Railway Cup for Connacht and we didn't do any good. I got tired of it then.

'I had to leave Galway because I had no more work. We had a brother at home and I knew he was getting the place. I said I'd go to Tipperary to work. I played for Lorrha. In '48 I was picked on a Tipperary team for the first time. I hoped I'd be picked for 1949 and I was picked. We had to meet Cork in '49 in the first round in Limerick. We drew the first day. We had to meet them again and it was a draw again. We eventually won. We got in the All-Ireland after and we beat Laois. We beat them well. That was the first medal I got for an All-Ireland, the medal for 1949.'

There are countless stories of great games and great saves involving Tipperary's Tony Reddin, although surprisingly few relate to his All-Ireland final appearances. In 1949, '50 and '51 Tipperary and Tony Reddin stormed to three All-Ireland successes, defeating Laois, Kilkenny and Wexford. The match against Laois was a stroll, with a score of 3–11 to 0–3. The contest with Kilkenny was a dull affair, with the narrowest of victories achieved by 1–9 to 1–8. Although he delivered an inspirational performance in the match against Wexford, the final score of 7–7 to 3–9 told its own story.

In those three finals Tony Reddin won his full complement of three All-Ireland medals. Although those medals are treasured possessions, it's to the great Munster contests with Cork that Tony's thoughts return time and again. Those were mighty hurling battles, fiercely fought and passionately contested. They were also the days when opposing forwards came charging in, their shoulders, knees and hurleys wildly flying, with the goalkeeper the target of their suspect intentions. Goalmouths were battlefields, with shoulders crashing, the crunch of bones and the crack of hurleys. A goalkeeper needed sharp eyes, cold concentration, a fearless demeanour and razor-sharp reflexes. As it happened, they were qualities possessed in abundance by Tony Reddin.

'You had to keep watching the ball the whole time,' Tony says. 'You'd block the ball. You'd touch the ball with the hand and bring it down to the chest. If the ball hopped on the chest you'd have to catch it again. You'd then side-step and clear it down. I never blocked it down on the ground. I didn't like that because the forwards coming in would score on you. I'd block it and get it in my hand. Then you'd go out to the left or the right. If you cleared the ball in the middle, you'd be blocked down in the net. I'd pass to Mickey Byrne and he'd pass it up to Jimmy Finn, up along the wing.

'The goalie would want to be very fit. You'd want to have a mighty side-step as you'd see the forwards coming in. If I'd see the forwards coming in I'd side-step and I'd see the two or three going in the net. I'd go out and clear the ball then. You'd have to work the head that time. I'd want to train three nights a week at home and three nights a week in Thurles. You'd want to be very fit to jostle and everything. If they were too near you, you'd have to jostle them. Then I'd pass the ball to John Doyle or Tony Brennan and let them play it off down the wing.'

Nowhere did Tony Reddin display those qualities to greater effect than in his battles with Cork's Christy Ring. Opposing each other were Cork's deadly sharpshooter and Tipperary's ice-cool goalie. They were friends in Munster Railway Cup sides but adversaries when playing for their counties. Throughout the late 1940s and '50s they faced each other year after year, before crowds of 40,000 and 50,000. Some were league matches, others crucial Munster championship jousts. Tony describes one of those contests where he saved a Christy Ring rocket from all of nine yards.

'He gave me a mighty shot, I'll never forget it,' Tony recalls. 'There were five or six on the ground and Christy Ring was on the ground. Christy Ring stopped the ball and he turned around and faced me and shot. I just blocked it up. I didn't know where the ball had gone. It had gone straight up in the clouds. Didn't I watch Gerald Murphy looking up! So I got the ball coming down in my hand and I gave it to John Doyle. John Doyle went out and cleared it. Then the Cork forwards flattened me down on the ground.

'I didn't know what happened. Was it in or what? A Corkman on the sideline wanted to know: "How did you stop that ball from Christy Ring from nine yards? That was the best shot I ever saw." Christy Ring gave me a great shot and he had a woeful shot. You couldn't watch him. He was a mighty man. He was a mighty forward and hard to watch.'

Another of Tony's Christy Ring memories involves the 1949 Munster first-round replay between Tipperary and, yet again, their old foes from Cork. That day, Cork's Mossie O'Riordan delivered a pile-driving shot which ricocheted back into play. The advancing Ring declared it a goal, clearly believing the ball to have rebounded from the woodwork at the rear of the net. In exasperation at the umpires' slowness to signal a goal, Ring flung his hurley to the back of the net. It was an act that may well have cost Cork a crucial goal, as a free for Tipperary resulted from his intemperate action.

'I didn't know what happened with the hurl in the net,' Tony says. 'I was watching the ball the whole time, with the Cork forwards coming in with Willie John Daly on one side and Paddy Barry on the other side. I was watching the ball and wondering would it go over the bar or would it be wide. I just looked up and I saw Ring fire his hurl and it was in the net. I got a fright and I stooped down and saw the hurl was in the net. "Oh, by God, that was Ring," I said to my own full-back, Tony Brennan, "don't do anything." I said: "I'm not going to let

him in for the hurl, I'm not going to touch the hurl. Let him stay out."
You see that was the good hurl and I thought if I gave it to him Cork
could win it. He got a new hurl and later he missed a free. He sent it
wide.'

Throughout his career Tony Reddin was known for his calm self-
assurance and his cool control under pressure. He was, people said, a
master craftsman applying his techniques with pride and precision.
The communication skills he displayed on the field also implied a high
level of understanding with his team-mates outfield. In truth, however,
what was little known at the time was that Tony was deaf and suffering
from associated speech limitations.

In his early years Tony's hearing condition severely curtailed his
ability to either hear or speak. He was good at lip-reading, although
people without teeth posed problems. Despite those difficulties,
however, few goalkeepers could boast a better knowledge of their
fellow players. Colleagues point to his remarkable relationship with
one of his backs, Tony Brennan, who had once played with him for
Galway. He also had a fine rapport with Mickey Byrne and John Doyle.
In addition, it undoubtedly helped that the teams he played with
boasted quality players like Pat Stakelum and Tommy Doyle, amongst
many others.

The team also devised secret codes for puck-outs, with players
scratching their heads to signal that they wanted the ball. One player,
Jimmy Kennedy, once proposed that he would tie up his bootlaces to
signal that the puck-out should come his way. 'Jimmy Kennedy walked
over by the sideline and he tied up his shoes,' Tony says. 'He'd be
watching me pucking the ball out. He kept away from Kilkenny by ten
yards and they didn't go near him. The very minute I pucked the ball
to him he got a lovely hop and snapped it over the bar. The goalie later
said to me: "That's a mighty puck, you've got great eyes."'

In 1950 Tony's ability to hear and speak improved when he was
introduced to his first hearing-aid during a trip to New York. It was
remarkably effective in one ear, although bulky and useless for hurling.
Needless to say it was an appreciable advance on the situation in
Ireland, where hearing devices were virtually unknown at the time. On
a further trip to New York in 1957 it was replaced by another smaller
and more compact device but by then Tony was at the end of his

hurling career. Thankfully, however, through hurling he had been introduced to the latest hearing technology and his condition improved with the years.

'I could hear the whistle,' Tony remarks. 'I could hear Tipperary talking and Cork talking in all those games. In 1950 I went to New York. There was no hearing-aid here in Ireland. I hurled over there and some Yank fixed up an old hearing-aid. The first time he gave me a free one. It was very, very good. I could hear everything with the pocket one. In 1956–57 we won the league and we went to New York in '57, and he gave me a different small one. It was very good again.'

By the mid-1950s Tony Reddin was fast approaching the end of his hurling career. To many observers it seemed that his time minding nets still had a long way to go but that was due primarily to his delayed start with Tipperary while in his late twenties, having previously served with the Galway juniors and seniors. After ten years in Tipperary colours, he travelled with his county to New York in 1957. Following the trip, having recently won his sixth league title, he hung up his boots and retired from the inter-county hurling scene.

'I'd got tired of it all,' Tony says. 'I played an awful lot of matches with the juniors and seniors of Galway and ten years for Tipperary. It was hard work there for ten years. I went to New York twice. I went to London every year for ten times. I had no days off. I always kept going. I went to New York then in '57 and I said that's the last match I was playing. I came home from New York and I played no more.'

Throughout his career Tony Reddin played with one of the finest teams in Tipperary hurling history. 'They were mighty hurlers,' he says. 'It was hard hurling. It was a hard team, with good hurling and great style. I never saw it so good.' He also played against some of the finest forwards the game has ever seen. This was the era of legends like Christy Ring, Jack Lynch and Nicky Rackard, all of them, at some stage in their careers, bearing down on Tony in the Tipperary goal.

'We had great backs and great forwards, all around the ground. We had deadly backs like Tony Brennan, Mickey Byrne and John Doyle. We had Pat Stakelum, Jimmy Finn, Tommy Doyle. Of the best forwards I saw, I think Jack Lynch nearly was one of them. Jack Lynch had a mighty stroke and Christy Ring had another. Nicky Rackard was good too, with a deadly stroke. I can't pick the best of the three of them. The three of them were very good. I could stop Mossie O'Riordan once and he had the hardest shot I ever saw. But I broke the hurl with the ball.'

In all, Tony accumulated three senior All-Irelands, six National Hurling Leagues, five Railway Cups and three Munster medals throughout his illustrious career. His highlights also include a valued U-14 medal won back in Galway. In recent times, however, came his prestigious selection on both the Team of the Century and the Team of the Millennium. In a position noted for the remarkable talents of players like Kilkenny's Ollie Walsh and Noel Skehan, those selections marked him out as the undisputed number one goalkeeper in hurling history. For a Galwayman, who starred with Tipperary and who now lives in County Offaly with his wife Maura, that's some record of achievement.

'I didn't think I'd get on that stamp,' Tony concludes. 'I was delighted. I don't know how I got it. I went to Croke Park and my wife was beside me. I thought: "Where are all the goalies?" There were none of them there, only myself. I didn't know who was going to get it. Would I get it the second time again? The first was in '84. We ate the dinner there and my name was called up. Maura hit my knee and said: "You'll have to go up. They're pulling down your picture there." I had to stand up beside the picture. I'd got top goalie again. I was delighted I got it. I was delighted with the way I got everything.'

6. JIMMY SMYTH

IT WAS SAID OF CLARE'S JIMMY SMYTH THAT HE WAS THE FINEST HURLER NEVER TO WIN AN All-Ireland medal. Described by Christy Ring as the best hurler of his generation, Jimmy, had he come from Cork, Tipperary or Kilkenny, would undoubtedly have experienced All-Ireland success. Instead, this talented hurler played with a Clare side trapped in the backwaters of the sport and was denied his rightful share of hurling glory.

In the place of All-Irelands, Jimmy ended his career with eight Railway Cup medals won with the cream of Munster hurlers, together with five senior county championships won with his native Ruan. He also shared in Clare's historic Oireachtas final victory in 1954 over a Wexford side that boasted the likes of Nicky, Bobby and Billy Rackard, Art Foley and Nick O'Donnell. Success it might have been, but it was scant reward for one of the greatest exponents of hurling skills ever to play the game.

For eight decades, including Jimmy's era from the late 1940s to the late '60s, Clare sank into hurling obscurity. Ever since their famous All-Ireland win of 1914, when they beat Laois by 5–1 to 1–0, the county were relegated to the role of perennial hopefuls in Munster hurling. 'Clare,' as Jimmy says, 'were worthy of an All-Ireland win in every decade but they weren't able to get there.' Instead, he adds: 'It took a man like Ger Loughnane to pull them out of the doldrums and give them the confidence that was needed to win an All-Ireland final.'

In 1995 Clare finally cracked the code and won both Munster and All-Ireland finals. After a gap of over 80 years, the county celebrated. Grown men cried, bonfires welcomed home the victorious hurlers, every town, village and parish celebrated the great event. Hurlers like Jamesie O'Connor, Ollie Baker, Brian Lohan and captain Anthony Daly became overnight stars. Clare did it again in 1997. For Jimmy Smyth, all those years of graft, of crushing losses, of hopes dashed by other counties, were finally brought to a close.

'The most enjoyable event of my life was the winning of the 1995 All-Ireland,' Jimmy says. 'It's something that you can't explain. All the frustrations, all the disappointments and all the walking home in sorrow were put aside. We no longer remembered the past; we remembered the present. We were there on top and that was great.

'As Anthony Daly said around that time, and I agreed with him: "We are no longer the whipping-boys." People frowned on that statement. They shouldn't have because if you asked anybody in Ireland, prior to 1995, would Clare win the All-Ireland final, they'd say they wouldn't. You'd get one-hundred-to-one against them.

'I remember a great friend of mine who was having a "do" down in Ennis and he spoke about the fact that the great days in his life were the day that he was born, the day that he was married and the day his first child was born. "Look it," I said, "why wouldn't you tell the truth that your greatest enjoyment, the biggest excitement of your life, was the day Clare won the All-Ireland in 1995?" "Well," he says, "if I was telling the truth, Jim, it was."

'It's a very funny thing too that, before 1995, when I'd be introduced as a Clare hurler, even though you'd be reasonably good, they'd always say: "Oh, yeah. Clare, yeah, yeah, yeah." Being a Clare hurler was frowned on and didn't mean that much really. But now that Clare have won two All-Irelands, having been a Clare hurler means that much more. It resurrected an awful lot of those old hurlers who were very good but never got the credit for it.'

Jimmy Smyth came from Ruan near Ennis, County Clare, where he was born in 1931. With an uncle who played for Clare and a mother who was a hurling enthusiast, it was understandable that he should shine at the sport at school and college level. He played for his native Ruan and he also attended St Flannan's College, Ennis, where he won three Harty Cups and three All-Ireland Colleges medals in the 1940s. Despite a late start, from the age of 13 he was already showing immense promise as a hurler.

'I never got a hurley until I was about ten years of age,' Jimmy recalls. 'A hurley was a luxury. I remember exactly the first day that I hit a ball in the air. I tried about 12, 14 or 15 times and I eventually hit it. I threw the stick in the air, ran in and told my mother: "I hit it." That was the first ball I ever struck in my life. After that, I always had a hurley in my hand. My mother, you see, was the kind of woman that wouldn't let you sit in a draught but when you were playing hurling you could play in a downpour and everything was all right.

'Then I played with the club and a peculiar thing at that time was that we hadn't many juvenile matches. Juvenile matches weren't arranged as they are nowadays. I only played one juvenile match in my life, at about ten years of age, and very few minor matches. Then I came to Flannan's and it was from there really and from the older players in Ruan that I learned my skills.

'When I went there first, about 1944, that was the first time they won the All-Ireland. At that time, they got in a man by the name of Tull Considine. There was a great, legendary family in Ennis called Considine. There was Tull and there was Brendan and there was Willie "Dodger" Considine. Tull, by the way, got a record score against Galway in the All-Ireland semi-final of 1932. He was way before his time. He was telling me things at that time that didn't arise until about 30 or 40 years afterwards. He knew every stroke of the ball.

'There were lots of things that I learned. I learned that a small little tip of a ball is as good as a big stroke. One time, when I played left half-back, I was hitting strongly but I realised that when you tipped the ball out of a fellow's way you were achieving the same thing. At least he hadn't got the ball. You also learned how to side-step. You learned how to tip a ball over an opponent's head. Then, more than anything else, you learned how to strike the ball well.

'I never scored until I was about 15 or 16 years of age. I scored my first points against Roscrea in an All-Ireland Colleges final. I scored five points that day. From that day onwards, once I got the confidence, I never went off the pitch without getting at least two or three scores.'

A deft and skilful hurler, from the age of 13 Jimmy Smyth attracted the attention of the Clare minor selectors. Conveniently born on 1 January, he says with a smile: 'I always say that my mother, being a great GAA enthusiast, registered me on the first of January knowing that I was born on the twenty-ninth of December. The first of January gave me an extra year as a minor; that's what gave me the edge.' In fact, that extra year ensured that Jimmy represented Clare minors for a record five successive years. It also helped draw the attention of the junior and senior selectors, who were soon seeking his services.

'I played my first inter-county match when I was 17. It was a wet day in Ennis, in the National Hurling League. I'll never forget that. I didn't get my place the following year. I played with Clare juniors in 1949. I probably would have got a senior place in '49 but the juniors were doing well so I was held back.

'We got to the All-Ireland junior final in 1949 and we were beaten by London and that was a bit of a disaster. That was a sadness, as well. We had many sadnesses in Clare hurling but that was one of the big sadnesses, even though it was only in junior hurling. Clare were winning nothing. We had to win something.

'It was very hard to keep going. It seems to a person who isn't winning that the GAA revolves itself around stronger counties. I always felt: "We're a little republic ourselves. We have to go and develop our own little support in our own county. We're not getting the publicity. We're not getting the acclaim. We're not getting the honour that the stronger counties are getting. We'll have to enjoy ourselves in our own area." That's where my own club came in. During my period I won five county championships with Ruan. That kept me going. Only for Ruan, I wouldn't be there at all.'

There were three crucial years in the mid-1950s when the legend of Jimmy Smyth was formed. The first came in 1953 when he demonstrated his extraordinary marksmanship with a record 6–4 score in the Munster championship against Limerick. The following year, 1954, much was expected of the promising Clare team and they delivered in the Oireachtas tournament with some style. Their opponents in the final were the form team of the mid-1950s, Wexford.

In the first drawn match in the 1954 Oireachtas final Jimmy Smyth showed his cool marksmanship with a crucial goal and a last-minute point to secure a draw and save the day for Clare. In the replay Clare convincingly defeated Wexford by 3–6 to 0–12. Considering the talent at Wexford's disposal, the result was quite remarkable. Remember that in 1954 Wexford began the first of three successive All-Ireland appearances, losing in '54 but winning in '55 and '56. Clare had defied the odds to win their first-ever Oireachtas title.

The following year, 1955, the Clare revival continued when the

Banner County fought their way to the brink of provincial greatness. In the first round of the 1955 Munster championship Jimmy scored the crucial point that condemned Cork and Christy Ring to a shock defeat. They maintained their momentum in the next round, defeating Tipperary. Unfortunately, the run came to a surprise end in the Munster final, when Clare and Jimmy Smyth succumbed to a rampant Limerick and returned home empty-handed.

'We had beaten Limerick by 10–8 to 1–1 in 1953,' Jimmy recalls ruefully. 'But this was a new team that came on in 1955, a team that was trained by Mick Mackey. They had an awful lot of young players, great players, and they annihilated us in the Munster final. It was quite possible that if we met them the following Sunday the result might be changed. But on that day they were vastly superior. Many of our team, including myself, I suppose, didn't play as we should have. But that's how it turned out and we didn't arise from that débâcle until 1995.

'Yet we had a very good team. We had top-class men, from the goalie up to the full-forward line. We knew that we were able to beat any team in the country. We trained hard and yet we didn't achieve what we set out to do. We did achieve it in the sense that any team that would beat Cork and Tipperary in the one year, at that time, were certainly worthy of an All-Ireland final. But this was a great Limerick team and, as I said, Clare had a team worthy of winning an All-Ireland final in every decade but they weren't able to get there.'

Despite his woes with Clare, Jimmy Smyth was selected on the Munster inter-provincial panel on 12 occasions. With Munster he won eight Railway Cup medals, playing alongside legends like John Doyle, Jimmy Doyle and Pat Stakelum of Tipperary, Phil Grimes and Tom Cheasty of Waterford, and Josie Hartnett and Paddy Barry of Cork. He also, of course, played alongside Christy Ring in many of those games with Munster, partnering him over a full ten-year spell.

'He fought for every ball,' Jimmy recalls. 'He had tremendous balance. He was able to strike a ball at the length of himself and the length of his hurley. The most difficult thing he did, and I think D.J. Carey does it now as well, is that he would come in with the ball on his stick and strike it with the same force as if he were standing. That's a very difficult thing to do. Carey shortens his grasp on the hurley but

Ring never shortened his grasp. It's a great skill. But Ring's great skill was his balance, his strength and his intensity.

'He shunned publicity but at the same time I think he liked publicity. He was on Des Ferguson one day in the Railway Cup and the heading in the paper the following day was: FERGUSON OUT-HURLS RING. He came to me. "Jim," he says, "did you see the heading in the paper, Ferguson out-hurls Ring? I saw Ferguson do nothing, did you?" He was concerned about the publicity he was getting.

'He was a very intelligent man. He was able to analyse a game from the beginning to the end. His analysis was always kind of different to other people. He concentrated on the referee and the type of referee that was there. He also concentrated on the type of player that was on him, whether he was left-handed or whether he was right-handed. He knew the game from top to bottom.

'I remember Jack Lynch saying one time that if he hadn't been good at hurling, or if he hadn't concentrated so much on hurling, he could have been a specialist in any field that he ever cared to take up. Jack Lynch, at the time, I think, mentioned surgery. He could have been a great surgeon. He could have been anything. Ring could have been top class at any other field that he would take up.

'He was a very human man, too. He came to Ruan in 1971 to open the pitch for us. A lot of stars came the same day. After the match, everybody was around Christy and he was avoiding the publicity, as he usually did. I said: "Come down to see my mother." He came down to my mother. She was sitting at the table, glasses on, grey hair. She said: "Hello, Christy, sit down, have a cup of tea, how are you getting on, how's the family, what are they doing?"

'They kept on at that for one half an hour and he was cosying up to her the whole time. It was so easy, away from the throngs. I was a stranger in their company. He was so happy. When he was going, he stood up and he said to her: "Do you know, missus, your son is the best hurler in Ireland." Now, I don't know whether he meant that or not but it was a lovely thing for him to say and my mother was delighted.

'John Doyle was also a giant. He was very loyal to his club and his county. We all applaud him for the eight All-Irelands and the 11 National Hurling League medals. Apart from that, he generated his own greatness, as every great player does. There were a lot of players playing with him when he won all those titles but I always said that he was great because he played for 19 years for Tipperary.

'He was also a great utility man. Tipperary were very lucky because when they had a weakness in one place they could slip Doyle into it. There's another thing that is never remembered: that in all those 19 years Doyle was never substituted and that's an extraordinary thing. That meant he never got an injury, so he was able to look after himself. That was a great skill.

'Jimmy Doyle was a miracle. He was able to score from any position. He was very skilled and had great control of the ball. He used to tip it around on his toes, get it up into his hand and slide it over the bar. He had a very small hurley, which a child could play with. It's extraordinary the force that he was able to put into every shot that he hit. Jimmy Doyle would never take a point if a goal was there to be taken. Like Ring and Rackard and Carey and Langton, the great players never went for a point when there was any chance at all of getting a goal. That's their greatness.

'It was very difficult to come out and stand beside those fellows and say you're just as good as them. It's very difficult to do that, to come out of a club and out of Clare who were defeated either in the first or second round. You went into a Munster final and you were usually defeated. I found it very hard to find my feet initially, until I suddenly realised, talking to all these fellows, that they were human the same as the rest of us.

'As well, playing with Munster you didn't get many passes of the ball at that time. In 11 years that I played with Munster, I only got two passes. I thought that I was required to pass the ball, which I did very often. But then eventually I was going for my own score as well. It was selfish enough. There was a lot of rivalry between the counties at that time. Cork mightn't want to see Tipperary getting the limelight and Tipperary mightn't want to see Cork or the smaller counties getting the limelight. That is the way it was. There wasn't that much combination play in the Railway Cup in my time. You had to fight for your own ball and get your own score.'

In 1967 Jimmy Smyth retired from hurling having given almost two decades to the game at the highest level. Throughout his career he was best known as a right corner-forward, although he played in numerous positions including both wings, centre-field and in the backs. Since the mid-1960s he continued his involvement with the GAA, working as Executive Officer at Croke Park. He remained in that position until 1988, when he retired.

Following his retirement, Jimmy studied philosophy at Trinity College, Dublin, where he completed his BA degree in 1993. He then studied the hurling and football ballads of Ireland and completed an MA in 1996 on the songs, poems and recitations of Gaelic games in Munster. He also published comprehensive compilations of the poems, ballads and recitations of counties Clare, Cork and Tipperary. Although still remembered as the greatest hurler who *never* won an elusive All-Ireland medal, he is regarded as one of the finest exponents of the game in Clare and Munster, where he has been honoured at county and provincial levels with Hall of Fame awards. He was also chosen on the Munster Team of the Millennium.

'Anything I ever got in life I got from the GAA. I would have been nobody only for the GAA and only for the skills that I displayed on the hurling field. I'd maybe be Jimmy Smyth the clerk or the administrator. But the fact that you have played at inter-county level gives you a kind of passport into every hurling county in the country. It's a funny thing that if somebody comes into my own area, and I know that they've played the game of hurling, I don't go back over their record. I don't research their character or anything like that. The fact that they've played hurling means everything and the fact that I've played hurling as well means everything to me.

'It has been a great lesson as well, in that when you went out there you played against the toughest men in the country. It's a great lesson in life afterwards. You see them coming to you and you're able to assess them immediately. You say to yourself: "Well, how would I treat him on the hurling field? Should I fear him or do I think he'll have enough courage to challenge me?" You have to make all these challenges off the field but you've already met them on the field. You've coped with them and when you meet these challenges off the field you tend to cope with them as well.

'To win an All-Ireland medal would have been OK. But I often remember there was an Olympic athlete, Armin Hary was the name of the fellow. He had won the 100 metres gold medal and then he wouldn't go in the 200 metres, even though he was probably favourite for it. His coach said to him: "This medal will be fading away in your drawer and nobody will have any concern for it in years to come. What they'll remember is the fact that you didn't run in the 200 metres final for your country." That's what an All-Ireland medal meant to me. It's not the medal; it's the winning of an All-Ireland title for the people of Clare who were following the team down the years. What I regret is all the people that I know who were following the Clare team and who never lived to see the winning of an All-Ireland final.'

7. BILLY RACKARD

A BLACK-AND-WHITE SNAPSHOT TAKEN OVER A HALF A CENTURY AGO DEPICTS THREE brothers leading the Wexford team prior to the 1951 All-Ireland final. Those three brothers, Nicky, Bobby and Billy Rackard, were achieving a memorable high point in their personal and hurling lives. Nicky captained the side. Led by the Artane Boys Band, he was followed by Bobby and Billy. A fourth brother, Jim, sat on the Wexford subs bench.

Their mother, for the one and only time in her life, had come to watch her sons play. Alongside her husband, she sat in the Hogan Stand clutching rosary beads. A family epitomising the hurling traditions of Wexford had, for one brief day, symbolically come together at the epicentre of hurling: Croke Park on All-Ireland final day.

That September day in 1951 Wexford were appearing in their third final in less than a year. They had already lost an Oireachtas final to Galway in late 1950. Galway were the winners again in early 1951, this time in the National Hurling League final. Yet, despite those defeats, it was clear that Wexford's momentum was building and a new hurling power was about to emerge.

In the following years the purple and gold of Wexford would appear in an extraordinary succession of All-Ireland, National Hurling League and Oireachtas finals. At the heart of that revival were Nicky, Bobby and Billy Rackard, whose time as a threesome at the pinnacle of hurling began at that memorable All-Ireland final against Tipperary in 1951.

'It was unique for us because my mother didn't want to look at matches,' Billy recalls. 'Both she and my father were in the old Hogan Stand and the three of us marched in front. It just happened that way. Nicky was captain at the time, as Rathnure had won the championship the previous year. Bobby hopped in behind him and I happened to be next. Jim was a sub that day. I can't recall anybody saying: "You go in number three." And my mother was up in the stand saying the rosary, although it didn't do us any good.

'My mother had often talked about an uncle of mine who played on the Wexford team that won four All-Irelands in a row at football. They had played in six finals and he played in one of them. I heard her tell stories that she went to see him play. But with us she kept away from it all. She wouldn't even get involved in conversation.

'Funny, though, she used to go down to Tramore, she loved Tramore, and she'd be sitting down there at that lovely wall. The matches would be on the radio. There were all kinds of women there. Apparently, if she heard derogatory remarks about Nicky from one of those women, she couldn't contain herself. She'd lambast some poor woman, saying that Nicky Rackard was not a blackguard or whatever was being said about him.

'My father was mildly interested in it. Of course, when he discovered he had three or four sons playing, his ego got the better of him and he used to go along. He was very quiet but he'd be listening to what people were saying and if somebody said something wrong about his sons he would correct them.

'At that time we had very little experience of Croke Park and it was quite frightening. I remember my mouth going dry. I got the "frighteners", I have to say. I should have been taken off. I shall never forget it. The occasion got to a lot of us. There were some very mediocre players with our team, including myself.

'The poor fellow who was in goal that day, Ray Brennan, was very inexperienced. We had about four goalkeepers through that campaign. My brother, Jimmy, was one. Art Foley, who returned to be our number one goalkeeper, was another. That was a bad way to be going into a final. As it was, our goalkeeper just wasn't up to it, although he did stop a few good shots.

'Tipperary were very good. They were vastly experienced. They had Paddy Kenny, John Doyle, Pat Stakelum, all those lads. They were a magnificent team. They were going for three in a row and we were absolute rookies. But it was a benchmark in our desire to achieve better things, which we felt would come.'

Prior to 1951, the last time Wexford hurlers appeared in an All-Ireland senior final was at the close of the First World War. Back in 1918 a Wexford selection faced Limerick's Newcastle West and even then they lost badly by 9–5 to 1–3. In the intervening years the Model County was little known for its sporting success. But in 1951, at the dawn of a new half-century, all that was about to change with a vengeance.

In an extraordinary two decades from and including 1951, Wexford contested nine All-Irelands, winning four. They appeared in eight National Hurling League finals, winning three. They also became regular contenders in Oireachtas finals, appearing in 12 up to 1972. As if by some magic formula, the fortunes of hurling in Wexford had been ignited at the start of the 1950s.

Like most revolutions, however, Wexford's transformation into a hurling power came from slow and cautious beginnings. Nowhere was that gradual evolution more clearly evident than in Rathnure GAA club, which catered for the Rackards' home town-land of Killanne. In 1940, early in the Second World War, Rathnure won its first junior hurling title. Featuring a family of rising young stars by the name of Rackard, Rathnure eventually went on to great success, winning its first senior county title in 1948. A hurling dynasty was about to take shape.

'You must remember, in the war years there was no other distraction. You had no other outlets. There was no table tennis, no lawn tennis, there was no television. There was very little money around then, too. It was our whole being, to an extent, to have hurley sticks and to get out there and play. It was our entertainment.

'I can remember getting up on a Sunday and you dare not miss first mass at seven o'clock. You'd come back and you'd gobble down your breakfast. You'd run out to the field and you'd hurl until you were called for your dinner. You'd gobble that down and run back out. You'd be called in for your supper. You'd gobble that down and you'd be back out literally pushing the darkness off the sky for another bit of hurling. That was the way it was. It was our entertainment as much as anything else.

'It was a very different society. You went to the park to play for pleasure. People talk about skills. We'd spend eight hours in the park.

Today, lads would go up for an hour and a half. They'd get fit but we'd be there all day. If we went to the beach, we'd bring the hurley sticks with us. We played hurling all the time because there was nothing else to do. There would be some wicked tussling. The pecking order was established there. That's how you learned the tricks of possession and dispossession, hooking and blocking, and the intrinsic things of hurling. You can't teach skills; that's my own belief. You have to fight with your siblings or fellow youngsters and hold your own.'

First came Nicky Rackard, the eldest of five boys in a family of nine, who was born in 1922. A strong and inspirational full-forward, Nicky hammered in goals and points and came to hurling prominence in the 1940s. An instinctive goal- and point-scorer, he became one of the truly great legends of Wexford hurling.

Next came Jim, a mainstay of the Rathnure club, who played in the half-forward line and also in goal. He was regarded by many as the finest hurler in the Rackard family. A Leinster senior hurling medal winner, he also togged out as a sub in the 1951 All-Ireland final.

The legendary third brother, Bobby, was born in 1927 and became one of the greatest backs in hurling history. Of all the brothers, Bobby, another mainstay of Rathnure and Wexford, was the only one to make it on to the Team of the Millennium.

Fourth in line came John, who at six foot three and 13 stone as a minor was a likely candidate for a successful hurling career. However, despite a brief appearance in the Rathnure colours, his hurling career never took off. Quite simply, John and the sport of hurling didn't see eye to eye.

Last of the five boys came Billy. Another great defender, he was born in 1930 and went on to a long and distinguished career in Rathnure and Wexford colours. Having played up to 1964, he became the last of the Rackards to appear in the purple and gold of his county.

'Contrary to what people might believe, Nicky's halcyon days were in the middle and late '40s, not when we broke through,' Billy recalls. 'Nicky was totally different in the '40s. He played midfield at that time and was very athletic. He was a terrific overhead striker, a great ground striker. Afterwards, when he put on a bit of weight and moved into full-forward, he reminded me of Muhammad Ali and the "rope a dope". He'd hang around the square and he had what all of the great forwards have, a fixation about firing a shot in a split second. The top-class player will do it instantly. The middling player will touch the ball two or three times, then he's in trouble. But Nicky had that. Once he caught it in his fist, the shot was gone.

'I remember him in 1944 when he literally beat Kilkenny on his own with ground hurling down in New Ross. But he went through a difficult time in his life and he put on weight. He wasn't the other Nicky that was there in the '40s. Bobby and I didn't put on weight, which can be a hell of a problem. If you get over 30, especially, and you're losing that little edge and the old avoirdupois is catching up with you as well, you have another problem altogether.

'Bobby was a phenomenon in the sense that he had extraordinary strength, although you'd never suspect it looking at him. He was a pale-faced guy. He had terrific reflexes, you couldn't sell him a dummy. Talk about the expression that's used today, "shutting them out". By God, he'd shut you out. He was unfortunate with his legs, he lacked a little bit of speed, but once he got a ball few men would take it off him. He'd make room, he'd come around with his elbows and if he caught you with his elbow you'd think it was a hammer hitting you. He had incredible strength and he'd lash it then upfield.

'I wouldn't have Bobby's strength. I wouldn't be able to do what he'd do. I'd do a little bit of it. I wasn't exactly a weakling but I would be depending on getting out in front and taking the ball with me. Bobby would trap it and people would say: "Why don't they stop him?" I mean, it was ridiculous, he'd just trap it, give a shift this way and that way, throw it up in the air and just whack it up the field. He was quite extraordinary in that way.

'My skill was catching the ball coming at me from very high. In the 1956 All-Ireland, when I was playing on Josie Hartnett, the first three balls that came down were coming in high. The Corkmen hadn't twigged it yet, really, or what the antidote to it was. I put up my hand and caught it a couple of times. I'll never forget Christy Ring, Lord have mercy on him, he came out and screamed at Josie Hartnett and he said to me: "That isn't hurling at all, it just isn't bloody hurling at all." So it worked well at times. But I'd put Nicky at his prime equal to Bobby. I wouldn't put myself in there. I learned a lot and I had a good long career. I played championship for 15 years and I played more games for Wexford from 1950 to 1957 than any other player, which is indicative of a little bit of talent. But I wouldn't compare myself to the others.

'Lots of people would tell you Jim was the best hurler of the Rackards. But he was a lot smaller in stature and he wouldn't be robust enough. He had plenty of skills. He played in the Leinster final in 1951. But he wouldn't focus on the game and he wouldn't train. John was a hell of a fine fellow. He was a bigger man than Nicky, an imposing fellow when he grew up. However, Bobby, Nicky, myself and Jim could ride horses, any kind of horses literally. I rode in point-to-points myself, so did Nicky. But put John up on a horse and he'd fall off the other side. He was left-handed and he just wouldn't react. You could push the ball back between his legs and he wouldn't cop on to it. He just didn't have the right reflexes.'

The rise of Wexford and the Rackards to national prominence took a while to accomplish. They lost to Galway in the 1951 National Hurling League decider and to Tipperary in the 1951 All-Ireland final. They narrowly lost to Tipperary in the 1952 National Hurling League final. They lost again, this time to Cork in the 1954 All-Ireland final, when the Rebel County were on their way to a famous three-in-a-row.

The mid-1950s, however, marked the watershed in Wexford's quest for All-Ireland glory. In 1955 they beat Galway in the final, winning by 3–13 to 2–8. The following year they turned the tables on Cork, beating them by 2–14 to 2–8. Just to confirm their arrival, they also won the National Hurling League in 1956. Furthermore, they rattled off three Oireachtas titles in 1953, '55 and '56.

The county of Wexford had never seen anything like it before. They travelled from farms, factories and fishing villages, from the far reaches of Hook Head, from the towns of Gorey, New Ross and Enniscorthy in support of their team. Great names entered the Wexford vocabulary: the Rackards, Nick O'Donnell, Jim English, Art Foley, Padge Kehoe. The golden age of Wexford hurling had arrived.

'It was tremendous. It was on a par with anything you can see today. You may not have had as much bunting or present-day flags or adornments flying. But I shall never forget the crowds coming back. You couldn't get into Wexford town. I mean, people talk about the present day and the massive crowds. They were there then, too. And all the black Morris Minors! It's rather interesting to look at pictures; they were all black cars and very few women. It's amazing if you consider there were 70,000 and 80,000 at the finals. Every car you looked into, there was hardly a female in it. Look at the scene today, it's very different.'

Wexford's pursuit of hurling success continued as the 1950s and '60s progressed. They won a further National Hurling League title in 1958. That year they also appeared in another Oireachtas final, where they lost to Galway. In 1960, with Nicky and Bobby departed, they won another All-Ireland, defeating Tipperary by 2–15 to 0–11. They confounded the sceptics, taking on the traditional counties with a brand of hurling never before seen in the game.

'We've been looked upon as great hurlers. I wouldn't concur with that. We certainly were achievers. But in the art of the game, we adopted different tactics to those the real classy players used, like lovely overhead striking and ground play. It wasn't beyond us but we didn't go in for it in games. We started a new thing, which was standing all-square and plucking the ball out of the sky at the last second. That was new. I think we invented that. It's all the ploy now, they're all putting their hand up. But that was really the gambit that we employed. We wouldn't be noted for ground hurling or for good overhead striking, although we certainly were good strikers in the sense that we had long deliveries. Every time we got hold of it, it went way upfield.'

Of the three prominent Rackard brothers, Nicky and Bobby were the first to retire. They quit in 1957, having won two All-Ireland medals, the first in 1955 against Galway and the second in 1956 against Cork. At the time of his retirement, Nicky was in his mid-thirties and very much in the twilight of his career. Bobby's departure followed a farm accident which resulted in major damage to his ankle tendons and ligaments.

Billy continued to hurl, eventually captaining both Rathnure and Wexford. He shared in Wexford's triumph in 1960, when the Model County beat Tipperary by 2–15 to 0–11 in that year's All-Ireland final. Two years later, in the 1962 All-Ireland, he captained his county when a famous Tipperary side took revenge for their earlier defeat and narrowly squeezed past Wexford by 3–10 to 2–11. By then, however,

Billy was moving into his thirties and the end of his career was also drawing near.

'I was captain that day in '62 and we had the beating of Tipperary but, I have to say in fairness, they were probably the better team. Tragedy struck us early. I wasn't well. Sometimes, no matter what you do or how you train, you're just not right. I knew I wasn't right. I was playing on Mackey McKenna and I couldn't handle him. In the first two minutes of the game I went out, someone climbed up behind me and I fell flat on the ground. My hand went out and McKenna let fly. He was in the course of pulling on the ball and he burst my hand in pieces.

'I was in plaster for eight months after it. And I played the full match that day! I remember going to the doctor and saying: "There's something wrong with my hand." I often think about it. He said: "Ah, you're all right." He didn't even look at it. I scored a point from a seventy with one hand afterwards. If I had been taken off, I think we might have won it. Nick O'Donnell, God be good to him, mishit two balls. Something strange happened. I've never seen O'Donnell do it before. Before that game really got under way, Tipperary were two goals up. That was a marvellous game. It was a wonderful game. It was one game that really saddened me to lose.

'I played again in '63 and had a very good year. I think I played in '64. Then I opted out of a few matches. Several newspapers rang me and I said I didn't know what I was doing. I didn't realise it but I was never going to play again. I had had enough. I didn't realise I had played so long. A lot of people tend not to notice you if you're the younger brother of two powerful men, as Bobby and Nicky were. When I say I played for 15 years in the championship, people say: "You what? I only thought you were there for a few years!" I realised that at the time and I thought it was time to get out.'

In the following years Billy Rackard's brothers, who were part of the great Wexford teams of the 1950s, passed away. Jim, the sub of 1951, died of cancer while still in his fifties. Bobby died in late 1996. Billy's wife Jill, also in her fifties, died of cancer. Nicky Rackard, one of the most revered and enigmatic hurlers in Wexford history, was another to die a tragic death. A heavy drinker for much of his life, he too developed cancer and passed away at the age of 53.

'Nicky died a terrible death. The man was eaten alive and he never complained. It was extraordinary. I mean, Nicky had a problem but he got it all together. At the end of his days he was a successful vet and a good man to train racehorses; he had some very good wins. He came down to me one day and I said: "What are you doing with that handkerchief around your neck?" "Ah, nothing, it's nothing," he said. It was summertime. The whole family was suspicious. I asked a sister. I said: "What's wrong with him?" Sure, he had cancer and for a whole year he never told anybody, I think. But it really went through him quickly, very quickly.

'During the last couple of years of his life Nicky was a prominent member of Alcoholics Anonymous. At his funeral it was astounding the thousands of people who turned up. You couldn't get into the town of Bunclody, you had to park outside. The massive gathering of people was more than a testimony to his hurling prowess; it was equally a tribute to the extraordinary work he had done with Alcoholics Anonymous. He pulled so many people out of the fire, so to speak. His leadership qualities came out again. Nothing today gives me more pride or pleasure than when someone crosses the street to me and says: "I would not be walking up here today only for Nicky."'

Throughout the 1950s and '60s the Rackard name became synonymous with Wexford hurling in the same way that legends such as Ring, Mackey and Keane became inextricably linked with Cork, Limerick and Waterford. Undoubtedly, Nicky was the star performer, a player who once scored 7–7 against Antrim but whose skills were diminishing when he amassed his medal collection in the 1950s.

Bobby was the strong inspirational back whose reliability, style and talent ensured his selection for the Team of the Millennium. Billy was the rock-solid defender who received an All-Star Hall of Fame award. He is also the last remaining member of a dynasty that energised and helped define Wexford hurling in the greatest era in the county's hurling history.

'One of the prizes or nice things is that people remember you with affection. I think that old team is remembered with affection. The first thing people often do is they look at the All-Irelands we won. We won three, we played in six and we were unlucky not to win two more, although I'm sure Tipperary and Cork wouldn't agree. But forget about the All-Irelands. You take Oireachtas finals, we appeared in a lot of those. They were great games with 30,000 and 40,000 in Croke Park.

'Then you had the inter-provincial games, which we took part in as well. And, of course, there were many National Hurling Leagues. Just look at the record of that team, how long they were knocking on the door. Padge Kehoe, at 35 years of age, was a star in 1960 and 1962. That shows a man with talent and there were several like him. I'd have to rate the team very highly. I mean, you look at a present-day team and they win an All-Ireland. They're suddenly gone from the scene. The bulk of the Wexford team remained on for 10 or 12 years.

'I'm not one for looking at, or staring at, medals. They could be anywhere, inside in Wexford as far as I know. However, I made a scrapbook years ago. I got a big hardback book the size of the *Irish Independent*. I had a fellow working in the business with me and I said: "Look, I have this pile of newspapers and I want you to stick them in that book." I actually got two books because there was quite a lot. I said: "Make sure they go in in chronological order." He did it. But sure, nobody looks at them except maybe an odd fanatic ringing up looking for them.

'But when my four girls were growing up, the first one came home from school one day and she said: "Daddy, did you play football or something?" She asked me rather quizzically. I said to my wife: "The time has come to produce my scrapbook." I produced the scrapbook and they all got down around it and started looking. "My God, you've got very old," was the first comment.

'To a large extent, I think we are remembered because of the name we had, Rackard. We are the only family who carries that name in Ireland. I'm often asked: "Oh, you're from Wexford?" "How do you make that out?" I ask. "Oh, you're with the hurlers, aren't you?"' If we were Doyle, Hennessy or Murphy, it wouldn't be the same. It's a factor in perpetuating our name, I believe. On top of that you had four of us, while three of us reached very dizzy heights in the game. That, plus the unusual name, is a down payment on longevity, I think, isn't it?'

8. JOHN DOYLE

IN 1949 A TEENAGE JOHN DOYLE, FROM HOLYCROSS, COUNTY TIPPERARY, TRAVELLED TO Dublin to play in his first All-Ireland final. That year, as the 1940s came to a close, the nation was a very different place indeed. Only months before, Ireland's first President, Douglas Hyde, had died. At Easter, Éire officially became the Republic of Ireland. John A. Costello's inter-party government held power. Éamonn de Valera and Fianna Fáil sat in opposition. A TB epidemic raged throughout the country. Meanwhile, two counties, Laois and Tipperary, prepared to face each other for the very first time in an All-Ireland hurling final.

In September 1949 almost 70,000 Laois and Tipperary supporters travelled to Dublin to watch their teams compete. They were led by captains with exotic names: Ruschitzko for Laois and Stakelum for Tipperary. However, that September day few observers could guess that a 19-year-old player, John Doyle from Tipperary, would eventually secure a record eight All-Ireland senior hurling medals (a record shared with Christy Ring) and a record 11 National Hurling League medals. Won during Tipperary's golden years from 1949 to 1967, those medals would define the career of a legendary defender who played with some of the finest teams in hurling history.

'The big All-Ireland was 1949 because it was the first one I played. I was only 19,' John recalls. 'Being selected for my county was all my dreams come true. I lived hurling, I ate it, and for me it was everything. I was very lucky to be on that team because it was a great team. We had some fabulous players. We had a big, strong team and I can always recall one of our great coaches saying: "A good small man is good but a good big man is better."

'I was so young at the time I didn't know what it was all about. It was just another game to me. I can remember going to Dublin on the Saturday by train and we were taken by bus out to Blackrock College. That was all new to us: the city and all. Here was this starry-eyed young fellow going out to Blackrock. We were all in bed before 11 o'clock and up the following morning and looking out into the sea, watching the steamers going across to London. It was all new to us. Then we went through Dublin on the bus and saw all the colours. I knew then that the moment of truth was at hand.

'There was something special about Croke Park. In my opinion, you haven't really played if you haven't played in an All-Ireland final in Croke Park. It's the biggest moment in anyone's life, in sporting circles in the GAA. I remember back in 1949 it took me about five or six minutes before I even realised where I was. That was my first time ever in the big time. There was a big crowd there that day and Tipperary hadn't won an All-Ireland for about four or five years. Expectations were high but all I was concerned about was that I wouldn't let the side down.

'Luckily enough, I had a few fellows who had been around a while and they were able to steady me down a bit. In the dressing-room it wasn't so bad until a fellow from Croke Park came and gave us the word to be ready about ten minutes before we went out on the field. It's then it hits you: this is it. The few moments in the dressing-room before you go out onto the field at Croke Park are the most tense moments of your life. You want to do justice not just to yourself but to your county. Your whole year's training depends on 60 minutes, as it was at the time. All your dreams could be shattered in 60 minutes. But luckily enough we won on that occasion.

'The 1949 All-Ireland final itself became a bit anticlimactic because we won it rather easily. Laois, at the time, hadn't been one of the most prominent counties in the country. But, fair play to them, they were there. They went along with Tipperary for a while but eventually Tipperary pulled away from them and we won easily in the finish. Then, when it's all over and you've won, there's the backslapping and all that. It's an occasion you'll remember for the rest of your life.

'There was great excitement because Tipperary hadn't been setting the world on fire for years. Because people had been starved for a while, it was marvellous. People came in from around the country into the town to meet us when we came home. There were the old fire-bangers under the train. It was great.'

From a farming background in Holycross, County Tipperary, John Doyle emerged on the hurling scene in the mid-1940s. An only child, whose mother died the week of his birth in February 1930, John was raised by his father and soon took an interest in hurling. In 1946 he played his first minor matches for his county, losing to Dublin in the 1946 minor All-Ireland final. The following year he was back again with the Tipperary minors who this time won All-Ireland honours, crushing Galway 9–5 to 1–5. A strong, accomplished defender, this teenager from Holycross inevitably caught the eye of the Tipperary senior selectors and he was soon showing his talents on the national hurling stage.

'In rural Ireland we hadn't much more to do at the time. Every time you'd pass a crossroads there would be young fellows hurling in a field. I started in national school and I progressed from there to the CBS in Thurles. There were some very ambitious Christian Brothers there. You either hurled or you didn't. But I loved the game, even from a very early age. When I was going for the cows, or here or there, I'd carry a hurley around with me. That's the way it was. My whole social life was taken up with it and it progressed from there.

'At that time, players like Johnny Ryan and Tommy Doyle were boyhood heroes of mine. I was always imitating them when I was a young fellow. I really wanted to play for Tipperary, if I could at all. It was one of my dreams that I would play in an All-Ireland final. I suppose it's everybody's dream to play in Croke Park. You really haven't arrived if you don't play in Croke Park and I dreamed that some day I'd play there. I was encouraged by a lot of people who were involved in the game around here and I showed a bit of promise when I was young. I have a lot of people to thank for that.

'I was very ambitious at the time. I always felt I could make it. When I was a young fellow, I remember going down to the hurling field in Holycross, cycling down on the bike. I remember passing a particular fellow on the road who was a better hurler at the time than I was. He said to me: "John, where are you going? You're only killing yourself. Rest yourself. What are you going down killing yourself for?" For two seconds I very nearly turned around and went back. But I got up on the bicycle and kept going. If I had turned back it would have changed my whole life.'

John Doyle was selected for the Tipperary senior championship team in 1949, eventually playing in that year's victorious Munster final against Limerick. He also, of course, appeared for the Tipperary seniors in the 1949 All-Ireland final, defeating Laois by 3–11 to 0–3. With John Doyle in defence, that formidable Tipperary side went on to huge success, winning their second All-Ireland in a row in 1950, defeating Kilkenny 1–9 to 1–8 and making it three in a row in 1951 by crushing Wexford 7–7 to 3–9. John Doyle had won his first three All-Ireland medals in a side that combined strength and style and that caught the imagination of the Tipperary public.

Following that team's demise came a revival in 1958, which brought medal number four for John Doyle following Tipperary's victory over Galway in the 1958 All-Ireland final. Once that team declined, it was followed in the 1960s by one of the greatest teams in the history of hurling. That 1960s Tipperary side swept all before it and, in doing so, transformed the game of hurling.

In the 1960s Tipperary won four All-Irelands, in 1961, '62, '64 and '65, thereby securing four more medals for John Doyle. That side also appeared in the 1960, '67 and '68 All-Ireland finals, where they were beaten by Wexford, Kilkenny and Wexford respectively. The 1960s were the years when great players such as Waterford's Tom Cheasty and Phil Grimes, Kilkenny's Ollie Walsh and Eddie Keher were at their peak, while Cork's Christy Ring and the last of the Rackard brothers of Wexford were reaching the end of their hurling careers. But it was the flair and power of Tipperary that dominated hurling and, year after year, it seemed their inalienable right to play in All-Ireland finals at Croke Park.

'At that time, very few teams would stand up to us. We had the likes of Liam Devaney and Donie Nealon. They were outstanding players. We had great forwards like Mackey McKenna and Seán McLoughlin. They were all big, strong, physical guys. They were dedicated and they were all winners in their own right. That is the hallmark of any great team. I think there are very few teams around who would live with them at any time.

'Jimmy Doyle was exceptional. He was brilliant for years and got scores that other people could only think about. Jimmy was outstanding, a deadly enemy of mine at club level but off the field we were great friends. He was probably Tipperary's greatest forward for 15 or 20 years. Once Jimmy got a free, you could be putting up the flag before he even hit it. I remember we played Kilkenny in an All-Ireland semi-final and of our 1–13 I think Jimmy scored 1–8. He was a match-winner on his own.

'I remember in the 1961 All-Ireland final, I was playing one of the Boothmans. It was the first time I ever saw a fellow out hurling and wearing an earring. I think they were of German extraction. He gave me a bit of a roasting that day and we were terribly lucky to beat Dublin. We won, just by a point. In fact, I often felt sorry for a great friend of mine, Des Foley, who was playing on the Dublin team. They were devastated afterwards. But we had a very strong team and we went on to win the following year.

'In 1962 Wexford had a powerful team, with big, powerful men. As a matter of fact, that Wexford team should have won more than they did. It was a great final, man-to-man stuff. It was a heart-warming final to have played in. There was no dirty play, it was all played in a great sporting spirit and the crowd loved it. But we came out lucky in the end and we just made it.

'It's a funny thing to say but a time came in Tipperary when we were winning so much that they were really hoping we'd be beaten. They got fed up of us winning. I remember a time coming home from an All-Ireland final and, honest to God, there was hardly a murmur. People were there to meet us off the train and we went down to the cathedral with the usual ritual. But it had all gone very quiet and low-key. People got tired of us winning. It was just expected and that was it.

'I was moving on age-wise. I gave them a certain amount of confidence at the back. We had a couple of big fellows there like Kieran Carey, Michael Maher and myself. We were the hierarchy at the back and we gave great confidence to the rest of them. I suppose you gain in experience as the years go on. We were also winning and that kept us going.

'As you get older you realise what you're walking into and you get even more nervous. I was always tense but I feel that if you're not tensed up then you're no good. My knees would be rattling going out into Croke Park but then after five minutes I was away. Once I got a feel of the ball, a touch of the ball, no problem. But beforehand, in the dressing-room, I'd be eager to get out. I'd be like a horse in a stall, just mad to get it all over with.

'When you run out first, the crowd is intimidating. But once you get involved in the game you wouldn't even know they existed. You wouldn't notice them, you wouldn't even hear them. Once you got into a team like I was with, playing with them for years, the crowd didn't bother us. The more that was there, the better we played.'

Throughout his hurling career John Doyle and the Tipperary senior side were preoccupied not just with All-Ireland success but also with their titanic battles in tough Munster championship matches. In all, John won 10 Munster senior hurling medals, having played in 14 finals. However, the most fondly, or at times bitterly, remembered finals involved games between Tipperary and their neighbours Cork, played before capacity crowds of over 60,000.

Witnesses to the five successive Munster finals up to 1954 involving Cork and Tipperary testify to the astonishing atmosphere, the extraordinary skill and passion of the play and the remarkable competitiveness of the contests. Tipperary, with John Doyle the pillar of defence, won two of those Munster finals, while Cork, with the legendary Christy Ring at the height of his powers and fame, won three. That rivalry continued into the 1960s, when both counties fought to escape the confines of Munster and secure a place in the All-Ireland final at Croke Park.

'There was an intense rivalry between Tipperary and Cork on the field of play and Munster finals were special occasions in themselves. I remember playing Cork down in Limerick and there were 60,000 or 70,000 people there. At that time, there was more noise at matches and people got worked up more. The occasions were unbelievable. I'd have to give Cork people one thing: they are great people to accept victory and defeat.

'I remember the 1960 Munster final with Cork in Thurles. That was the most titanic battle we were ever in. I remember playing that day on Paddy Barry. I was playing in the half-back line at the time. We did the honourable thing. When we had a row during the match we put the hurleys down, had a boxing match, got finished with it, picked up our hurleys again and went away and not a word about it. Nowadays, you'd get the red card for that. But I think the crowd loved it.

'Christy Ring was also a very special man. He was able to inspire the rest of the Cork forwards. Apart from his brilliance as a forward, he was their leader. The crowd on the sideline were behind him as well. The funny thing about him was that the older he got the better he got. He was better in his latter years than when he started.

'I can remember an occasion when we played a Munster final in Thurles against Cork. We beat Cork that same day after an intense battle. I remember passing down that evening and Christy Ring was standing outside Hayes's Hotel, himself and I think it was Terry Kelly of Cork. Most fellows that evening would be drowning their sorrows, drinking after being beaten. But Christy Ring was outside discussing with your man the way they'd have to start again next year. Next year was already on his mind and the game wasn't an hour over. How do you keep down somebody like that?'

Included among John Doyle's medal collection are the record 11 National Hurling League medals he won throughout his illustrious career. The sheer number of medals alone illustrates Tipperary's dominance in the competition. Having won the National Hurling League in 1949, Tipperary went on to win it again in 1950, '52, '54, '55, '57 and '59. They dominated again in the early 1960s, winning in 1960, '61, '64 and '65. Along the way they defeated teams like Cork, Kilkenny, Wexford and Waterford, not to mention New York. Tipperary's trips to America, coming as they did at a time of high emigration, rate among John Doyle's fondest memories of his hurling career.

'They were fabulous trips. A lot of us would never have left Shannon, never mind going to the States, only for us winning the league finals. I can remember the first year we went, in 1950. I was very young at the time. I remember boarding the plane at Shannon Airport and flying away for a while, maybe an hour or an hour and a half. Next thing I heard over the speakers: "Fasten your seat-belts, we're now coming in to land in Shannon." I thought we were nearly ready to land in America and we were back in Shannon. We had developed engine trouble. I'll never forget it.

'That time we went, there hadn't been a team out in the States for years. When we arrived in New York there must have been a couple of thousand there to greet us. This was all new to me then as well. I remember playing in the Polo Grounds, in front of a huge crowd, and we only won by two points. There were more Irish going out there at that time and playing hurling. They had a very good team and Gaelic Park was abuzz with excitement. All the Irish would meet there on a Sunday. If you were over in New York and you wanted to meet somebody or find out about somebody, you went up to Gaelic Park on a Sunday and you would find out about them. They were outstanding trips.'

In 1967 John Doyle played in his last All-Ireland final, against Kilkenny at Croke Park. It was 19 seasons since he had donned the Tipperary colours as a teenager in his first All-Ireland final, against Laois. By now the wear and tear of a career stretching back to the 1940s was taking its toll and, like John, the team facing into the 1967 final were past their best. Of the 15 Tipperary players marching out at Croke Park in 1967, 8 were over 30 years of age. Perhaps understandably, John Doyle's hopes of winning a record ninth All-Ireland medal were shattered by Kilkenny on the Croke Park turf.

'An awful lot of people wished me well but it was a dying kick for me. I was gone. I played the final and all good things come to an end. I had my mind made up beforehand that I was going, one way or the other. I think it was a disappointment to a lot of people who would have liked to see me get it. But I didn't take it too badly because I felt I got enough out of it.

'However, records are there to be broken. I hope someone from Tipperary will be the first to do it. I can't see anybody doing it in a hurry but the record will be broken eventually. I mightn't be around to see it but it will happen for definite.'

From 1949 to 1967 John Doyle became known as one of the finest and most fearless defenders in the history of hurling. Regarded as a 'hard man' of the game, he excelled for his county at left corner-back and right corner-back and as a left wing-back. Of the ten senior All-Irelands he played in, he won eight, thus sharing with Christy Ring the all-time record of eight All-Ireland senior medals won on the field of play.

A Texaco Hurler of the Year award-winner and voted on the Team of the Century and Team of the Millennium, he also won an all-time record of 11 National Hurling League medals to add to his Oireachtas medals and his Railway Cup medals won with Munster.

Finally, after a career touching on three decades, John Doyle retired following Tipperary's defeat in the 1967 All-Ireland final. Since then he has lived with his wife Anne in Holycross, County Tipperary, where his career began all those years ago.

'I was gone 36, just 37 years of age, and, for God's sake, it was time to give it up. Here I was, going for 17 or 18 years, never at home on a Sunday, gone every second weekend some place, flying to London, going to New York and I missed all that. I missed that terribly for about 12 months and then it wore off. I made a clean break and got out of it at club level and the whole lot. There was no point in hanging on. I achieved as much as I could expect and that was it.

'I had played in three eras with three different teams. They were all great in their own right, with different styles. I think of all the great players I played with. You just couldn't take it for granted that you were going to be on a team. No matter how good you were, there was always somebody to take your place. At one stage during my career with the Tipperary team, I will say this much: the second best team in Ireland were the Tipperary subs. We had eight or nine fellows in the subs that would walk onto any team. That's what makes a great team.

'One of the great regrets I have is that I possibly let hurling take over my life too much. I'm sad to say that even though I loved the game and I was brought up in the atmosphere of the whole thing, it took over my life a bit too much. I neglected things that I should have done. I went away training when maybe I should have been at home. That would be the only regret I have about the whole thing.

'I met some great characters down through the years. I made a lot of friends and, of course, a few enemies as well. I'm sure that when I die a lot of people will come to the funeral to see am I really dead, am I really gone down? But, having said that, it's a great game. It's been a part of my life. The GAA to me wasn't just a game: it was an institution, a way of life. I'm grateful to the GAA for that.

'I was just very lucky. There were fellows who were as good and better than I was and they never won a medal. I could name players who were terribly unlucky. Take the likes of Jimmy Smyth, of Clare, for instance. There was a great player but he wasn't lucky enough to be on a winning team. There were numerous fellows like him. They weren't there at the right time. I was there at the right time. That was it.

'As for the medals, up to a few years ago they were in a jam jar but then I gave a loan of them to one of the banks. They had some display and they brought them back in a nice frame. The eight All-Ireland medals are now on loan to the museum in Clonmel. The others I don't look at too often. They are memories, as far as I am concerned. But it's nice to have them.'

9. TOM CHEASTY

A CURIOUS EVENT HAPPENED DURING THE PRE-MATCH PROCEEDINGS AT THE 1957 ALL-Ireland final featuring Waterford and Kilkenny. Sharp-eyed observers might have noted an extra player marching in Kilkenny colours to the sound of the band. The presence of that sixteenth man wasn't an attempt by Kilkenny to stack the odds in their favour. Instead, it was British actor John Gregson togged out in Kilkenny colours while being filmed in his new movie role.

The name of that film was *Rooney*, an unlikely feature starring Gregson as a Dublin Corporation dustman and part-time hurling hero with an eye for the ladies, and Barry Fitzgerald playing a bedridden man. Apparently turned down by Waterford, the movie's director George Pollock had secured permission from Kilkenny to film his lead performer marching along with the team. The plan for the following week was to re-shoot action close-ups with the players and to cut them in later to the final production.

A week, however, is a long time in sport. By then a devastated Waterford side were little inclined to return to Croke Park, the scene of a heartbreaking defeat by Kilkenny. With just over ten minutes left to play, Waterford were leading by six points and seemingly heading for victory. Having cruised to the All-Ireland final by defeating Limerick, Cork and Galway, a rare victory seemed in their grasp. But they crumbled with the end in sight and lost a thrilling All-Ireland by one cruel point. The final score that day: Kilkenny 4–10, Waterford 3–12.

'It was supposed to be that John Gregson wanted to walk along with the Waterford team,' Tom Cheasty, Waterford's legendary centre-forward, recalls. 'For some reason or other we didn't think it was the right thing to do. He marched around with the Kilkenny team to get the shots they wanted. We went up then about a week or so after the All-Ireland to do shots to put into the film. I think some of the lads couldn't go back there. They were so disappointed.

'We came from nowhere and were within a point of winning. We had it won and we lost it in the last seven or eight minutes. They got a couple of goals and we were a point behind. But Ollie Walsh won it for Kilkenny. That just shows you the way the play was going. Ollie had the game of his life. I remember hitting the ball from about 14 yards out and he saved it. He was only a young fellow at the time but he was like lightning. Ollie was not alone stopping the ball but he was coming out, about 20 yards out. He had a big bearing on that game. That was probably his greatest game.

'It's easy to criticise a ref but they don't do anything for the underdog. I remember Mick Flannelly being in possession of the ball maybe a minute or a couple of seconds after the 60 minutes. That was a 60-minute game. He was in possession of the ball out under the old Cusack Stand. He was in a position to have a go for a point. The whistle went. It was a bit of a heartbreak because when you only come from no place you wonder will you ever come again.

'If you're one of the big three – Cork, Tipperary and Kilkenny – you're going to be there every three or four years anyhow. It's not that much of a disappointment to the players that are used to winning. But it's a terrible disappointment when you're not used to winning. You're going to say to yourself: "We'll never be there again."'

Despite the disappointment of 1957, Tom Cheasty went on to unprecedented success with the great Waterford side of the late 1950s and early '60s. For a small county better known for its hurling passion than its hurling success, the years ahead brought glories rarely seen in Déise history. Led by centre-forward Tom Cheasty, that Waterford team beat all before them, including the mighty Kilkenny, Tipperary and Cork. They also won All-Ireland, National Hurling League and Oireachtas titles in one of the most competitive eras in hurling history.

Born in Ballyduff in 1934, Tom Cheasty took to hurling and football as a youthful spare-time activity. Brought up on a farm, the 'iron man' of hurling, as he would later be called, developed a strong, muscular frame that would soon terrorise opposing defences. A Waterford minor in hurling and football, he played at wing half-forward for the hurlers and full-back for the footballers. By 1954, although just leaving his teens, his skill, turn of speed and sheer physical strength were spotted and he was soon a Waterford senior.

'My mother was a Kilkenny woman and my aunt was married to an old Kilkenny hurler, Martin Murphy. We used to spend a lot of our holidays over there, including weekends and all of our summer holidays. When we were young we'd be over there and Martin Murphy would bring us off to All-Irelands. He was a fanatic about hurling. That was one of the reasons I became interested in hurling because I wouldn't have any hurling tradition in my own family.

'Ballyduff is my own parish and would have a fair tradition of hurling. We won a championship in the early 1900s and we had a good enough team in the 1940s, '50s and '60s. I would have friends and neighbours at home who would be into hurling and I could go out in the evening and play with them.

'I think I was the kind of person who would be good at games. I was fairly good at football and I was fairly strong and fairly agile. In the opinion of a lot of people I mightn't have had any exceptional skill as a hurler. But I was fairly athletic, fairly strong, so that would be where I was coming from as a player. Maybe I wasn't a wonderful hurler but I was fit. I trained very hard. I had a good turn of speed and good stamina, and I had a reasonable amount, not a wonderful amount, of skill.

'I played minor when I was only 16 but I didn't have any great success. I wasn't a great minor and there was no U-21 team then. However, one day I was inside in the Sportsfield, Walsh Park, and Waterford and Kilkenny were playing and a few fellows didn't turn up. They were stuck for players and I'd been playing reasonably at junior level. Somebody knew I was at the match and they came out and asked me would I tog out. That's when I started playing senior inter-county hurling. That was towards the end of 1954, maybe going on into 1955, and it took off from there.

'In 1956 I played well against Cork in Fermoy. I remember it was a warm day and the Fermoy field was as hard as a rock. We were a bit unlucky to be beaten. I was playing on a young fellow called Mick McCarthy and I was only 22 at the time. But this chap was only 18 or

19. I wasn't very experienced myself but he was only out of minor, so maybe I was lucky that day.

'I remember Willie John Daly was playing corner-forward and they brought him back to play centre half-back in the last 20 minutes or so, to shore up the team. They beat us that day by a few points and I think Christy Ring scored a couple of goals. That was my first experience of playing against Ring. He was quiet for most of the game but he was one of the men that beat us in the finish.

'At the time, they used to pick two teams: Ireland and the Rest of Ireland. I was picked on the Rest of Ireland team and I remember scoring. I was playing on Billy Rackard and he was having a good game. So I was put in playing corner-forward on Bobby Rackard and, for some peculiar reason, I scored three goals on him. It was just pure luck, I'd say. He wasn't bothering. That was my first breakthrough, in terms of getting recognition.

'After 1956 I remember John Keane was thinking that maybe we had the makings of a reasonably good team, the kind of team where fellows would believe they had a chance of winning. That's an important thing with any team, to believe that you have a chance of winning. He had a good effect on the team. He was responsible, as well, for getting the team going, giving the team a bit of confidence. He knew he was a man that could do it himself and he was a man that gave the team something to look up to.'

Led by the legendary John Keane, the Waterford team of the late 1950s produced some of the finest displays of fluid, skilful hurling ever seen in the province of Munster. An exponent of fast, quality hurling, Keane added a sense of confidence and self-belief to great players like Frankie Walsh, Phil Grimes and Séamus Power of Mount Sion, Donal Whelan and Austin Flynn of Abbeyside, John Kiely of Dungarvan and, of course, Tom Cheasty of Ballyduff. Generally small in stature and with an abundance of natural talent, the side hustled and harried, played beautiful hurling and, in the process of doing so, destroyed the highly fancied, traditional counties of Munster and elsewhere.

Following the All-Ireland defeat of 1957, John Keane rallied his troops and prepared for a further assault on the championship. Although crushed by Tipperary 4–12 to 1–5 in the 1958 Munster final, the team returned the following year full of vim and determination. They turned the tables on Tipperary in the Munster semi-final, defeating the champions by the stunning margin of 9–3 to 3–4. Then, in the Munster final, they got the better of Cork, defeating the Rebels in an all-action game by 3–9 to 2–9.

'We met Tipperary in the first round and that was a famous one. We gave them a right beating in Cork. Then we played Cork in Thurles. Back in '57 Christy Ring was injured and the Cork fellows were saying: "You beat us but we hadn't Christy Ring." Christy was back for '59 but Joe Harney played him very well that day. Christy didn't have a great input to that game at all, for some reason. At least we beat them with Christy and all. We put paid to the idea that we wouldn't have beaten them if they had Christy Ring.'

With 74,000 spectators jammed into Croke Park, the stage was set for a pulsating 1959 All-Ireland final between Waterford and their victorious opponents in 1957, Kilkenny. That day, in September 1959, people travelled en masse from Waterford by road and rail, by farm truck and bus, to witness Waterford's best chance of All-Ireland success since 1948. For the first time in history television cameras were present, courtesy of the BBC, with the station's eminent commentator Kenneth Wolstenholme there to record what became one of the finest finals in history.

The result that day was a draw, with the score level at Waterford's 1–17 to Kilkenny's 5–5. The replay in October was an equally riveting affair. This time packed to the rafters, with a crowd of 78,000, Croke Park witnessed an initial burst of Kilkenny enthusiasm and all looked lost for the men from the Déise. However, inspired by two goals from the bustling Tom Cheasty, the Waterford team went on to record an eight-point victory, defeating Kilkenny by 3–12 to 1–10. The great team of 1948 had been matched by a new generation of Waterford legends.

'Ah yes, it was a great feeling, no doubt about it,' Tom Cheasty recalls. 'We weren't that far away from 1948, 11 years like, and there was some bit of a connection between '48 and '59. It was great. It was great for the people of Waterford, coming back to the city and to a great reception. I remember going up to Dungarvan and we had a great old time.

'I think we were brought into Guinness's and into Jacobs. I remember Fad Browne, from my own parish, coming out and talking about it. He would be Tony Browne's grandfather. He was a Ballyduff man and he referred to the fact that he was delighted to see a Ballyduff man playing a big part. Fad was a great hurler, probably the best Waterford hurler that didn't win an All-Ireland. Ah, it was good. For youngish fellows, anyway, it was good.

'There was hardly a weak link on that team. We had Ned Power in goal. Ned had a great year that year. Then we had Joe Harney, John Barron and Austin Flynn, a great full-back. Mick Lacey, who has passed away since, played a great game that day. Martin Óg Morrissey was at centre-back. Jackie Condon was there. Phil Grimes and Séamus Power were centre-field. Then there was Frankie Walsh, myself and Larry Guinan in the half-forward line. Mick Flannelly, John Kiely and Tom Cunningham made up the rest of the team.

'The Dungarvan area was well represented. You had Ned Power, who went to Tallow but I'd always call him a Dungarvan man. John Kiely and Tom Cunningham also came from Dungarvan, while Austin Flynn and Donal Whelan came from Abbeyside. Donal has passed on as well. Donal played a great game in '57 but he was only a sub in '59. He was injured or something. There are three members of the team that passed on, Phil Grimes, Donal Whelan and Mick Lacey, so it just shows you the way time passes on.'

With the dawn of the 1960s Waterford's run of success continued, thanks largely to the same core of players that won the All-Ireland in 1959. Their main adversaries in the early '60s were Tipperary, a team they lost to in the 1961 National Hurling League final but who soon met their match in the men from the Déise. The following year Waterford and Tipperary met in the Oireachtas final, where Waterford secured victory by 4–12 to 3–9. In 1963 the two met once more in a National Hurling League final, where this time Waterford denied their near-neighbours by a score of 2–15 to 4–7.

Ironically, that league final victory in 1963 became a bone of contention in Waterford hurling circles due to the suspension of Tom Cheasty. Tom made a major contribution in the epic home final against Tipperary, a game described as one of the greatest hurling classics by the eminent GAA correspondent John D. Hickey. However, following that match Tom was suspended for appearing at a dance in Waterford's Olympia Ballroom, which was sponsored by a local soccer club. Under Rule 27, otherwise known as 'The Ban', he received a six-month suspension and so missed the league final proper versus New York.

The implication of that seemingly cruel suspension was the denial to Tom Cheasty of a National Hurling League medal for a period of 33 years. As history would have it, that victory turned out to be Tom's one and only in the National Hurling League. It took until 1996, and the intervention of the Waterford GAA, for the wrong to be rectified and a medal to be issued by Croke Park. That retrospective medal was presented to Tom at a ceremony in Waterford in late 1996.

'I played the best game I think I ever played in 1963 in the league final against Tipperary and that was a good Tipperary team. Even John D. Hickey said it was one of the best hurling games he ever saw. The fact that I didn't get a medal didn't make much difference. It's what people know you did on the day that counts. As far as I was concerned, I played on the team. Most Waterford hurling supporters will know that I had a good game on the day and we beat Tipperary. That was the league final, as far as most people were concerned. But I got the medal a few years ago and I was glad to get it.'

In 1963 a confident Waterford qualified for a further All-Ireland final, their opponents once again being Kilkenny. They had already beaten Tipperary in the Munster final by the narrow margin of 0–11 to 0–8. However, that Waterford side still contained famous, although ageing, names like Power, Cunningham, Flynn, Guinan, Morrissey, Flannelly, Walsh, Barron, Cheasty and Grimes. Despite the passage of time, little had changed in the Waterford line-up and the end of an era was clearly in sight.

In retrospect, it's hard to believe that any team scoring six goals could lose an All-Ireland final. But in 1963 that's exactly what happened. Despite Waterford's remarkable half-dozen goals, they lost to Kilkenny by the margin of three points, the final result an extraordinary 6–8 for Waterford to Kilkenny's 4–17. Ruing a brace of late saves by Kilkenny goalie Ollie Walsh, the Waterford side of the 1950s and '60s had just witnessed its last hurrah.

'That wouldn't be a great memory for me,' Tom recalls. 'I remember I was put off in a club game. I missed out on a few matches and that probably made a bit of a difference. It's a match I suppose we should have won because we scored six goals and eight points. It was the highest score ever for a losing team in a 60-minute final. We had lost by a point in '57 and a goal in '63, so I suppose that's a disappointment. It's also a bit of a disappointment for the team that they didn't win a second All-Ireland.

'We were a bit unlucky that we were playing Kilkenny. Wexford were good at that time as well. It might have been better for us if Wexford had come through some of the years that we were in the final because local derbies are always hard to win, especially a local derby against a traditional team. You have three really traditional teams, Cork, Tipperary and Kilkenny. They always have a bit of a psychological advantage.

'Then we think that Croke Park is kind of the home ground for Kilkenny because they've been winning there as long as you can remember. It's a bit of an advantage for them to be playing there. We might have done better if we had, in some of the games, played against Wexford.

'After 1963 we played a few good matches in '64 and '65. We beat Cork in '67, who were the reigning All-Ireland champions from 1966. That would be one of my last inter-county matches. I remember I broke my finger inside in the Sportsfield the day we beat Cork in 1967. I wasn't able to play then for, I think, the Munster semi-final against Tipperary. Some of the lads were gone, like Séamus Power and Phil Grimes, who were a bit older than me. We just hadn't the fellows to take their place.

'We had a small pool of players and it's not easy. But the strong counties would have replacements. They'd have U-21 and minor teams winning. Kilkenny would be winning maybe an All-Ireland minor title every second year. That gave their players great experience of winning. I suppose we had about ten fellows nearly thinking of retiring and we just hadn't anyone to replace them.'

Of the achievements of that great Waterford team of the late 1950s and early '60s, arguably the most fondly remembered are the three Munster championship titles won in 1957, '59 and '63. Twice, in the 1957 and '59 Munster finals, Waterford dismissed Cork, by a score of 1–11 to 1–6 in 1957 and by 3–9 to 2–9 in 1959. In 1963 they beat a great Tipperary side by 0–11 to 0–8.

For a smaller county like Waterford, getting out of Munster represented a truly gargantuan task. They faced the might of great Tipperary sides bristling with talented players like Jimmy Doyle, Tony Wall, Liam Devaney and John Doyle. They also confronted powerful Cork teams featuring the likes of Paddy Barry, Willie John Daly and, of course, the great Christy Ring.

'The achievement of the team could be measured nearly by the winning of three Munster championships in the era of Christy Ring, Jimmy Doyle, John Doyle, Paddy Barry and Willie John Daly. It wasn't easy then. The team were something special for winning three Munster championships. I liked playing in the Munster finals. We generally had good weather. I can remember the sunny days. I suppose, as far as I was concerned, working on a farm, it was maybe a case of having the hay saved and Cork bet as well. That's where I'd like to be, back in the hayfields of long ago working hard. But those days are gone.'

Tom Cheasty retired from inter-county hurling having won virtually every honour in the game. Apart from his three Munster, one All-Ireland, one National Hurling League, one Oireachtas and five Railway Cup medals won with Munster, he also possesses five County Waterford Senior Hurling Championship medals captured after his inter-county days had come to a close. He won the first of those county medals with Ballyduff–Portlaw in 1970, the last with Portlaw in 1977.

His final county senior hurling medal was won at the age of 43. He also achieved a county title success with the Ballyduff juniors, whom he played with and trained at the age of 49, symbolising the dedication, natural skill, sheer determination and influential presence in Déise hurling of the great Waterford centre-forward, Tom Cheasty.

'Sport was the dominating thing in my life, hurling especially and football to an extent,' Tom concludes. 'Looking back, it has been the big thing in my life. I was maybe not successful in the same terms as, say, John Doyle, Eddie Keher and others. But I put a lot into it and I got something back out of it. I don't know whether I'd do the same again, maybe I would, maybe I wouldn't. But you don't get a second chance, so you make the best of it as it happens, I suppose.'

10. JIMMY DOYLE

WHEN TIPPERARY CAPTAIN JIMMY DOYLE WAS PRESENTED WITH THE McCARTHY CUP IN 1965 he turned spontaneously to face the crowd. Arguably the finest team in hurling history stood behind him. Thousands of overjoyed supporters were spread out before him on the Croke Park turf. Yet, among the blue and gold, one distant figure stood out in sharp relief. That solitary man, dressed in black, was Brother Boland of Thurles CBS. He stood alone, in dark contrast to the sea of glorious colour, silently watching his former pupil lift the coveted trophy.

Decades later that vivid image remains embedded in the memory of Jimmy Doyle. On that September afternoon in 1965 Seán McLoughlin had crushed Wexford with a two-goal blitz. John Doyle had collected his record eighth All-Ireland medal. Tipperary had won their fourth McCarthy Cup in five years. And the Thurles Sarsfields sharpshooter Jimmy Doyle had led his county to their twenty-first All-Ireland victory. Yet, for Jimmy, the defining moment of one of Tipperary's greatest days was the near prophetic emergence from the crowd of that powerful figure of Brother Boland.

'As a child I adored hurling,' Jimmy explains. 'My father was a shoe repairer and he made me a small little pair of hurling boots when I was about three. He put little cogs in them. I always loved hurling. As a baby, before I used to go to bed at night, my mother would have to come up to the sports field and shout at the gate to me to come home to bed. When I'd go home I'd bring my little hurleys with me to bed and I'd lie on them, like a mattress, and I'd have my hurling balls under my pillow. In the night-time my mother used to come into the room and take the hurleys and the hurley balls out from under me. But I'd wake up during the night and I'd bring the hurleys back into the bed with me again.

'During my schooldays I wasn't a great man for lessons. I wouldn't do my lessons and I always threw my schoolbooks into the corner. My mother did my lessons for me, while I'd get my hurley and ball and go up the field with my dog. I had a sheepdog. He was a very cute dog. He used to catch the ball and bring it back to me. He used to grab the ball, snap it in the air. I'd let on to hold the ball and he'd grab it. The dog and myself trained each other.

'When I'd be coming in from school, the dog would have the hurley in his mouth waiting for me. He'd know I'd be coming along. You see, a dog is very, very cute. That dog, Billy was his name, could outwit me when I'd throw the ball up to hit it. He was all the time watching the ball. When I'd hit it, he'd make a drive at it. But I'd try to outwit him and hold it or catch it. I'd be going to hit the ball and I'd pull back. I'd try to hold it or catch it before it hit the ground. If I didn't, he'd snap at it and have it got. That's where ball control came into my hurling.

'To practice frees I used to give hours and hours banging a ball over a big green door under the scoreboard at Semple Stadium, next to the Sarsfields field. I'd be on my own, banging a ball over the green door from every angle, running, hitting them backwards, hitting them sideways. I got my accuracy from that.

'When it came to the Primary Certificate, I knew I wouldn't pass because I hadn't any interest in school. All I wanted to do was hurl, hurl; that was my life. The morning of the exam, Brother Boland brought us into the classroom and he said: "Look, lads, every one of you is perfectly ready for the exam. But I'm afraid there's one man here and I think he won't pass. That's you, Jimmy Doyle." "Look, Brother," I said to him, "don't worry, I'll be all right." Now I went in and I didn't do that exam. I wasn't able. I hadn't the brains enough to do it because all I wanted to do was hurl.

'But Brother Boland said to me: "I will predict one thing and that is that you will play for Tipperary in a senior All-Ireland and you will captain a Tipperary senior All-Ireland team." Now in 1962 I did captain the Tipperary senior All-Ireland team but I broke my collar-bone and I was carried off. I was strapped to the stretcher in the dressing-room that day and the Knights of Malta told me I could receive the cup on the stretcher but I wouldn't do it. It was just one of those things; I wouldn't do that. Tony Wall, a clubman of my own and one of the greatest centre half-backs in my time, took the cup for me.

'However, in 1965 I captained the Tipperary team again and that year I got away with it. As I received the cup I turned around to give my speech and I saw Brother Boland right in front of me. He was standing in a patch of ground on his own, out behind the crowd. I took the cup, I went down to Brother Boland and I handed it to him. "Jimmy," he said, "my prediction was right. You were captain in 1962 and I was here. But you didn't receive the cup. Now I have all I want."'

No player encapsulated the grace and power of Tipperary hurling in the 1960s more than the Thurles Sarsfields forward, Jimmy Doyle. One of hurling's finest-ever sharpshooters, Jimmy could break the hearts of opposing defenders by picking off goals and points at will. An elusive player, his ease of effort and his seemingly casual ability to stop the ball stone dead made for a rare hurling style. Although he shared the limelight with great players like Tony Wall, Babs Keating, Donie Nealon, Mick Roche and John Doyle, it was the elegance, skill and goal- and point-scoring talents of Jimmy Doyle that caught the public's attention.

Born in the shadow of Semple Stadium in Thurles, from an early age Jimmy seemed destined to perform at hurling's highest level. With few academic leanings and virtually no interest in school, Jimmy modestly concedes that it was only on the hurling pitch that his talents shone. Obsessed by the sport, he became a central figure in the great Thurles CBS team that won all before it. By the mid-1950s it was already clear that a new teenage sensation was about to burst onto the Tipperary hurling scene.

'I started very young as a minor. I was only 14 when I played in goal for Tipperary minors. I never liked the goal. I always thought that if you let in a goal you'd always be blamed for it. I always wanted to get out of goal, which I eventually did. One evening, coming home in a car from the minor All-Ireland, I asked Brother Doody, the boss of the hurling team, would he put me in the forward line. The Thurles Dean Ryan team were playing the following Wednesday and he told me he'd put me out wing-forward. That's when I started as a forward. I never went back to goal.'

Jimmy Doyle, aged all of 14, played his first minor match for Tipperary in 1954. A loss to Dublin in that year's minor All-Ireland final was followed by a run of three minor All-Ireland medals in 1955, '56 and '57. In those three finals alone, Jimmy's scoring touches, honed in the fields of Thurles, were there for all to see. He scored 2–8 in the 1955 minor final against Galway. He scored a further 2–3 in the 1956 minor final, where Tipperary crushed Kilkenny. The following year Kilkenny were once again the victims when Jimmy produced an inspired performance, scoring another 1–3.

Elevated to the senior ranks in 1957, Jimmy's rise to prominence soon took off. That year, while still a minor, he scored crucial match-winning points for the senior side in their league final success against Kilkenny, eventually travelling with the senior squad to New York. By the summer of 1958, although just 19, the outstanding skill and talent of Jimmy Doyle had already brought him to the brink of national fame.

'I always wanted to win an All-Ireland medal and in 1958 we played Galway in the All-Ireland final. I was only 19 years of age. I was on Jimmy Duggan. Every player knows that there's a man on him and I knew Jimmy because I had played on him a few times before that. I was trying to figure out what way I would beat him or how I would get on with him. I had to do my homework and I trained hard for it. But Jimmy Duggan was a fabulous little wing-back, a small man, very fit. I had to try and outwit him but actually I didn't. I only scored five points that day and I scored three of them from frees. But we won, anyway, and I suppose to win your first All-Ireland is a big thing.'

The early promise of the 1958 Tipperary team received a set-back in the next two years. Unexpectedly destroyed by Waterford 9–3 to 3–4 in the 1959 Munster semi-final, the Tipperary seniors bounced back to reach the All-Ireland final in 1960. That year, however, a subdued performance by Tipperary resulted in Wexford's deserved victory by 2–15 to 0–11. It would take one more year for the ambitions of Tipperary's maturing team to come to fruition.

'In 1960–61 I broke my ankle. There was fierce pressure on me. I walked every day to the hurling field to try and strengthen up the leg. I thought I had my job done but Dr Herlihy, Lord have mercy on him, called three of us in for a fitness test. Tony Wall had a problem and also Kieran Carey. On the eve of going to Dublin for the All-Ireland Dr Herlihy told us to come to the hurling field, that he wanted to see how we'd get on with our injuries. I bandaged up my ankle and I went up to the field. I put on my hurling boots and my tracksuit and we hurled and I was grand. I felt grand and I thought I'd be ready.

'Then he told the three of us to trot around the field and when he'd blow the whistle we would sprint. He led us up to the top of the Killinan goal, we swung above the top and we came around, and the next thing he blew the whistle. The minute he blew it, I stopped. I got a crack at the back of the ankle. I knew the ankle wasn't right. It was then I knew I had a problem. Dr Herlihy said to me: "Jim, you stay here, stay put." He continued on with the two lads and they both passed their test. He came back to me and he told me to go to the sideline. I went to the sideline seats and he said: "Jimmy, I'm afraid you won't make it this Sunday, you didn't pass your test, your ankle is still bad."

'I burst out crying. I went home. I went upstairs. I didn't even say it to my mother or father. I went up and I lay on the bed and I cried like the rain. Dr Herlihy came to the house and he told my mother and father. He wanted to know where I was and they said I was upstairs. They called me down and he said: "Jimmy, you failed your test. I'm afraid you won't make it. But you can make it provided that you do what I ask you." I said: "That means I can hurl if I do?" "Well," he said, "it's going to be up to your father and mother and whether they'll give you the all-clear, whether they let you do what you want to do, what I want you to do. That is, I'll have to give you two injections before the game, to deaden the ankle up to the knee so that if you break the ankle again you won't know it."

'My father said to me: "Well, Jimmy, it's up to yourself. If you want to do it, you can do it." I was thrilled. I said: "No problem, I'll chance it." I did chance it on the day and by half-time I had got away with it. But about five minutes from the end the ankle started to get very sore. I pulled out over the line but Paddy Leahy told me to go back in because he said that Tony Wall and Kieran Carey had left the field. There were no subs left to go on. I turned to go back over the line. I was walking on my heel. Just when I turned to go back onto the field, the ref blew full-time. We had beaten Dublin, so I really got away with it with the help of Dr Herlihy.'

Throughout the 1960s Tipperary imposed themselves on the sport of hurling as no other county had ever done before. From their victory over Galway in 1958 up to 1968, they appeared in an unprecedented eight All-Ireland finals, winning five. In an era boasting great players like Christy Ring, Ollie Walsh, Eddie Keher, Tom Cheasty, Phil Grimes and Billy Rackard, few exponents of the game could match the skill, power and hunger of the great Tipperary side. Man for man, they matched the finest any other county could offer and they conquered great teams like Cork, Wexford and Kilkenny in titanic Munster finals and All-Ireland finals.

'I always said the 1964 team were the best Tipperary team of them all. I thought they were fabulous. There was an abundance of great players there and each and every player fought for their positions. Before the All-Ireland that year we were in the Spa Hotel in Lucan and we were in the lounge. Paddy Leahy, our manager, ordered a pint for everyone that drank a pint. But that was all they were taking; there were no second or third pints. It was going on half-past nine and we were all sitting back drinking an old lemonade or an orange when Paddy Leahy turned to us and said: "Now, lads, it's time to go to bed. We have something coming up tomorrow, it's time you went."

'There was no ifs or buts, everybody left the lounge and we all took to the stairs. The doctor was at the butt of the stairs with these tablets, small little tablets given to us to relax. Myself and Devaney always stayed together, we always slept together, we were like two brothers. We were going up the stairs together and I said: "I won't take the tablet, I'll fall asleep." Devaney said: "I won't take one either." We went up to bed, anyway, the two of us, and we lay in our beds and we were talking and talking. Suddenly I said to Devaney: "God, Billy, I'm just thinking here. You're playing left half-forward tomorrow and I'm playing right. If you let me switch to the left and you come to the other side, do you know something, we'll win this All-Ireland." He says: "Oh God, no, I wouldn't beat Martin Coogan. I'm not going over there, I wouldn't be able for him." Martin Coogan was one of the best left half-backs of all time in my books. "I won't beat him, either," I said. "All I want to do is win an All-Ireland."

'I got up out of the bed anyway and I put on my clothes. Devaney said: "Where are you going?" "I'm going down to Paddy Leahy," I said. I went down the stairs and I called Paddy Leahy in the lounge. Paddy came over to me and said: "Jimmy, why aren't you in bed? They're all gone to bed." "I know," I said, "but I want to switch tomorrow. I want to play left half-forward tomorrow because Martin Coogan is a ciotóg and he covers more from left to right than he does from right to left and he won't be able to hurl at the far side." "By God," says Paddy Leahy, "you're right." Up the stairs we go, the two of us, and he went in to Devaney lying in the bed. "Liam, you're playing right half-forward tomorrow," he said to Devaney. "Oh God, I'm not, I'm not able to play over there," Devaney says. "You'll do what you're told, you are going to play out there," he says.

'The following day the ball was thrown in and the two of us switched and I had five or six points scored before Martin Coogan was even switched to the other side. I always remember someone coming to the sideline roaring at Coogan to cross over to the far side. But Martin wasn't able to hurl at the far side at all and we beat Kilkenny wild. But I always thought that was a fabulous team and a clubman of my own, Michael Murphy, captained that Tipperary team, so it was a great honour for him.'

In the glory years of Tipperary in the 1960s Jimmy Doyle graced not only the national stage at Croke Park but also the many great hurling grounds of Munster. Epic Munster finals between Cork and Tipperary were fought in front of crowds of more than 60,000. The latter years of Christy Ring's career pitted his fading but still sublime scoring skills against those of his young admirer, Jimmy Doyle. As fate would have it, Jimmy played the day Christy togged out for his last Munster final in 1961, between Cork and Tipperary. The two great sharpshooters also shared the Munster colours in the annual Railway Cup campaigns, which netted a further bagful of medals for Jimmy Doyle.

'I always wanted to hurl with Christy Ring. Christy Ring was my idol. I often went down to the Glenmorgan House and I used to watch him, everything he did, even as he was spooning the food into himself. I got a great kick out of watching him. It was hard to believe, years after, that I played on the same team with him for Munster. It was fabulous. Ring was my God. I idolised Christy Ring. I suppose he was one of the greatest forwards of all time. I hurled with him umpteen times and I always thought he was a great man. Mick Mackey was a good one too but I didn't see him. He wasn't there in my time, although he was a selector on the Munster Railway Cup team. Among the great men there was also Phil Grimes, Séamus Power and Frankie Walsh of Waterford. Waterford had a great team. Back in the '60s Waterford would have won five or six All-Irelands only for us winning them.'

Like Christy Ring before him, Jimmy Doyle possessed the natural qualities of a genuine hurling artist. His speed, balance and variable pace, combined with a quiet temperament and intense dedication, produced one of the deadliest and most focused forwards in the history of the game. Technically brilliant, while possessing accuracy and precision honed throughout his early years, he focused on accumulating points, presuming – rightly, in his case – that the goals would follow. Not surprisingly, he ended up as leading scorer in five championship seasons and three National Hurling League campaigns.

'In my day I'd always take my point. If it was an easy free I'd just pop it over. If it was a hard one I'd try it, I'd go for it. If you take your points, the goals will come. It can happen too that you always drive the ball wide. It happens. It depends on the humour you're in. You can have a bad day or an off day. You can have a right good day too. It depends on the day.

'I often walked away from a free. I remember in a league final against Kilkenny in Croke Park, we got a free-out at the line. It was almost at the middle of the field and I called Donie Nealon over to take it. I don't know why I called him but I just called him. I looked at the post and said: "No, I'm not taking it." All of a sudden I called Donie and said: "Donie, come over and have a shot at it, try it yourself." As Donie was coming over I walked away but I turned and I came back to Donie and said: "Donie, no, I'll try it." I had lost my confidence at one stage and I regained it as I was walking away. When I took it there was no turn with it, it just went direct. I suppose it isn't a nice thing for a person to praise himself but I'd say it was one of the easiest points I ever scored and one of the hardest ones I probably ever hit. But that ball did go straight between the posts and, as I say, I'd always take a point because the goals will come.

'Your scoring ability can leave you too. I remember one time, 'twas in the '60s, no matter where I struck the ball it was tailing off to the left or tailing to the right. I didn't know what was going on. But my father used always say to me: "Go up to the field on your own and it will come back to you. Keep at it and at it and at it and you'll find your faults." I did find my faults: I wasn't following through. You see, it's like a golfer. I was cutting my stroke short and the ball was tailing and I didn't realise it. I found out from constantly shooting at the post, running and tipping and tapping with it, that I wasn't following through like a golf stroke. I was cutting my hurley short and wasn't letting it travel on. That's how I found my accuracy coming back to me. But I was always fairly accurate. When I had it in my hand I always knew what to do with it.'

In 1964 Jimmy Doyle won his fourth All-Ireland medal in Tipperary's destruction of Kilkenny by 5–13 to 2–8. A crowd of over 70,000 that day saw Jimmy contribute ten points to Tipperary's final tally. With their tails up, Tipperary returned to Croke Park the following year, where Jimmy secured medal number five in a 2–16 to 0–10 victory over Wexford.

Within a year or two, however, Tipperary's pool of players was ageing and the signs of the county's demise were beginning to appear. In 1967, with eight players over 30, Tipperary returned to Croke Park where they lost to Kilkenny. The following year they lost again, this time to Wexford, who avenged their 1965 defeat with victory by the narrow margin of 5–8 to 3–12. For Jimmy Doyle, the glory years were coming to a close. There would be one more All-Ireland victory and one last medal, in 1971, following which Tipperary's extraordinary run of success would abruptly end.

'I was nearly gone completely in 1971. I had disc trouble, back trouble, all my life. There was a man looking after my back called Jimmy Heffernan of Drangan. He used to put discs back for me. He put 14 of them back. Actually, as a young fellow I had a disc out and I didn't think I'd ever hurl. But my father brought me up to Jimmy Heffernan and he put two discs back in my back. They were out for years and they were always giving me trouble. They slipped from time to time. Jimmy Heffernan often went to matches with me, in his own car, and put back those discs for me. Even the day of a Munster final or an All-Ireland semi-final, he shoved the discs back for me at half-time or when I'd go in.

'But in 1971 things were starting to slow down a bit. I was getting on in years and, as I say, there's always a time to start and there's always a time to finish. I knew that time was coming. In 1971 I was a sub. I started in Killarney in a Munster final against Limerick but I was brought off because I had back trouble. The slower I was getting and the older I was getting, the more the back started coming against me. I suppose I was lucky to get in for ten minutes of the 1971 All-Ireland against Kilkenny. I was very, very lucky because my back was just about gone.'

Jimmy Doyle continued to play for Tipperary over the next two years but time was running out. By 1973 Jimmy was approaching his mid-thirties and the ravages of two decades of inter-county hurling, from minor to senior, were taking their toll. A litany of broken bones, involving fingers, ankles, knuckles, not to mention the collar-bone and back, was causing problems including premature arthritis. No longer able to command an automatic senior place, the end of Jimmy Doyle's career was now in sight.

'In 1973 I finished as the Tipperary senior goalkeeper. It was a bit ironic, really. I started in goal as a schoolboy. I played in goal for Tipperary minors. We played Dublin in the 1954 minor All-Ireland and I was in goal. But I couldn't ever understand how I ended up in goals in 1973. Tadhg Murphy of Roscrea went to England in 1973. Jobs were hard to get, even if you were a county player. He went off to England and Tipperary had no goalkeeper. They asked me if I'd play in goal for him. I didn't want to let him down, so I did.

'I played against Waterford in Thurles. I let in two. We beat Waterford, so we went on to play Cork in the Munster semi-final. Tadhg Murphy came back, so I asked the selectors to let him back in, let me out, that I'd go off the panel altogether. They wouldn't let me go. They held on to me but Limerick eventually beat us in Thurles in the Munster final. Actually, I was going in as a sub that day. Tadhg was nearly knocked out against Limerick. I went down in my tracksuit behind the goal ready to go in but it didn't happen and I was delighted it didn't. I was gone, so I retired then.'

In subsequent years Jimmy Doyle continued to live in Thurles, where he had attained legendary status for his exploits at school, club, county and provincial levels. Recognised as one of the finest forwards in the history of hurling, he was an obvious and automatic choice for the Team of the Century and the Team of the Millennium. Many of his remarkable collection of medals won at Munster, All-Ireland, Railway Cup and Oireachtas levels are displayed in the Thurles GAA Museum, where they remind visitors of the extraordinary career of Tipperary legend, Jimmy Doyle.

'Players are getting more out of it now. They have sponsorship and they have supporters' clubs. In our time we had nothing. If I had a pair of hurling boots and I burst the soles of them I had to go down and buy another pair. We used to put our jerseys into a bag and we used to use them the following Sunday for a league match. Now they have new jerseys, new tracksuits going out every day. We never had that. But, as I always say, I probably saw more than the generation today. I was in New York. I suppose I was in Gaelic Park, New York, about 17 or 18 times. I loved New York, going out hurling in 100 degrees of heat. I saw more out of hurling, I suppose, than they're seeing now.

'Unfortunately, I do have arthritis. I have it in my hands, all my joints, my knee and my ankle, my back and my collar-bone. But, I suppose, no matter what I have, if I were to turn the key and go back I'd still go back and do it all over again. I think it's a great game, it's one of the greatest games in the world and it's a lovely game to look at.

'Sometimes people come up to me and say: "Are you? Are you? You're not Jimmy Doyle? Are you Jimmy Doyle?" and "I thought you were a bigger man." I don't want to be remembered as somebody. I'm just an ordinary person. I go to mass on a Sunday like an ordinary person. As a matter of fact, if a person starts talking about me I start to sweat. I suppose it's an inferiority complex.

'But what I do love is to meet old players and to talk to them. I get a great kick out of meeting the likes of Tom Cheasty or Tony Maher or Ray Cummins. I have some great friends and, rather funny to tell you, four of my best friends are Cork people: Tony Maher of the 'Barrs, Ray Cummins of Blackrock, Denis Coughlan of Glen Rovers and Willie Walsh of Youghal. That's what I love, meeting old players and having an old chat and a talk.

'But as for a person to come off the road and ask me a question! This man recently came up to me with two Galwaymen and he said: "Come in here and meet Jimmy Doyle." "You're not *the* Jimmy Doyle?" one said. "I am Jimmy Doyle. Yes, I'm Jimmy Doyle," I said. "But are you the *hurling* Jimmy Doyle, the *Tipperary* Jimmy Doyle?" "I am," I said.

He nearly shook the hand off me. Actually, when he caught my hand I had arthritis in it and I let out a roar. I said: "Oh gosh, I have arthritis there." "Oh, Jimmy," he said, "I'm sorry." As I say, those things do happen and I suppose we have to accept it. It's one of those things as a sportsman. That's why I love the game.'

11. EDDIE KEHER

NO OTHER HURLER, WITH THE POSSIBLE EXCEPTION OF CHRISTY RING OR JIMMY DOYLE, brought the same fear or consternation to opposing defenders as Kilkenny's Eddie Keher. From his first games as a senior, Eddie took to scoring with an awesome intensity. He combined style with deadly accuracy. He scored goals and points with coolness and precision. Whether it was from frees or from the field of play, whether in challenge matches or All-Ireland finals, few could match Eddie Keher's record as a hurling marksman.

For ten years outright Eddie topped the national scoring tables. He scored 211 goals and 1,426 points for Kilkenny in 298 games. He also scored an astonishing 7 goals and 74 points in 10 All-Ireland senior finals. He hammered home 14 points in the 1963 All-Ireland final. He scored 2–11 in the 1971 decider, which remained an individual record until 1989. He scored 1–11 and 2–7, respectively, in the 1974 and '75 All-Ireland finals. To cap it all, he brought to free-taking a lethal consistency rarely seen in the game of hurling.

'Whatever skill I was able to develop, I developed down in the square in Inistioge with my pals,' Eddie says. 'We were always hurling, hurling against a wall, practising and competing with one another in the various skills of the game. I was on the U-14 team at the age of eight. I was young and small and I remember Martin Walsh, our teacher, used to have me out taking frees in the forwards. I suppose I developed as a free-taker from the very early stages of the game.

'Until such time as I went to college and came under the wing of Father Tommy Maher, my free-taking was just a case of up and take it. Whatever natural skill I had was sort of successful. But Father Maher fine-tuned that and gave me methods of making sure that everything was covered, ruling out any error that could come into the game. I found that very beneficial because, while it was all right in practice or in challenge games or in club games or whatever, when you came to the big days in Leinster championships or Leinster finals or All-Ireland finals you had to be sure mentally that everything was right.

'I always practised frees and practised them on my own. The evening before a match I always went out for three-quarters of an hour, or an hour, and just hit frees for that length of time. I could take a hundred or more frees during that period. So then I was mentally right for the game the next day. Even if I missed one or two early, I knew I had done the practice. If I felt myself going off with a stroke, a left-handed stroke or a right-handed stroke or a ground stroke or overhead, I just went out and practised and I got it right.

'I studied the game. I studied players and I tried to develop the best methods of doing the various skills, ones that I was comfortable with myself and ones that worked for me. Some may have worked for four, five or six years and if they started not to work I went out and worked on them again and maybe changed them. I studied the skills. I studied other players, what they did, and took what I could from what I saw happening all around me.'

Born in Inistioge, Eddie Keher caught the hurling bug from an early age. Inspired by living legends like Christy Ring and the Rackards, he admired the successful Waterford team of 1948. 'They were the first team I would have cut out pictures of and pasted in a book,' Eddie says. Those influences, however, were superseded by any young Kilkenny boy's natural obsession with the county's native sport.

'Our neighbours next door were the Ryans,' Eddie recalls. 'There were three brothers there and I could hear them playing inside through a sort of a wicker gate. I was probably only about two or three at the time. I had one sister and there was just two of us in the family. My sister would say: "Oh, they're the Ryans, they're playing hurling." That was my first memory of hurling. I was saying I'd love to know what's going on.

'Eventually, as we grew bigger, we got together playing. There's a square in the village and local youngsters used to go out there hurling. The older guys used to hurl there. Then, when they were gone, we'd come out and try to hurl. That was my first real introduction to hurling.'

Eddie Keher was soon playing with his local club, The Rower–Inistioge. He also played with St Kieran's College, where he won two All-Ireland Colleges senior medals. He further highlighted his remarkable hurling skills by playing four years at minor level for Kilkenny. 'I found it an absolute thrill to be wearing the Kilkenny jersey,' Eddie says. 'To be wearing the black and amber jersey and to be selected on a Kilkenny team was a marvellous experience. That time most of the minor games were played before the senior games. We were in the dressing-room next door to our heroes in the senior team.'

In 1959, at the age of 17, Eddie Keher shot to national prominence with the Kilkenny senior hurlers. He played in the minor All-Ireland final on 6 September. That same day the seniors drew with Waterford. The replay was scheduled for 4 October. In those four weeks Eddie moved from minor to senior, made his full senior début and appeared in his first All-Ireland senior final.

'In the first game against Waterford, Kilkenny were ahead and Waterford equalised with a last-minute goal,' Eddie recalls. 'It was a tremendous final, one of the best finals ever, I'd say. Johnny McGovern, who was an outstanding wing-back on the day, injured his shoulder and was extremely doubtful for the final. They may have also wanted to strengthen the panel but I was brought in anyway, first of all for training for the replay, which was absolutely unbelievable. You can imagine as a 17-year-old, not yet 18, being selected on the senior panel with fellows that I looked up to so much.

'They had a couple of matches between that and the replay. I remember playing my very first game with Kilkenny against Dublin. Kilkenny and Dublin were going out together on the field and I remember the great Des Foley of Dublin coming up to me and wishing me luck in the game. We had met at college level and minor level and I knew Des over the years. I thought it was a lovely gesture.

'We played Wexford then, in a game in New Ross. With those two matches I must have gathered a few Brownie points with the selectors. While they must have been concerned about my age, I must have been there or thereabouts to play in my first senior All-Ireland, especially with the fact that Johnny McGovern was doubtful. Actually, Johnny played. Even though Johnny was a back, I think the selectors had in mind that if he wasn't able to continue the game, or to play, they would move someone back and I would come in on the forwards. That happened. I think after about 15 or 20 minutes Johnny's shoulder gave, so I was called in. That was my first All-Ireland final.

'It was a big occasion, a huge occasion for me, and I suppose I was in awe of the situation. In some ways, maybe the match passed me by somewhat. Certainly in the first half I found it very hard to knit in with the rest of the team. But in the second half I more or less played my own game and did my own thing and it worked out reasonably well. I was reasonably happy even though we were well beaten by Waterford in the replay. I suppose at that stage, in contrast with my final days, you felt that an awful lot wasn't expected of you. The senior players would carry most of the responsibility. I was reasonably happy and I was delighted that I experienced an All-Ireland final. It was a massive occasion.'

It took until 1963 for Eddie Keher to appear in his second All-Ireland final. The opposition again were Waterford. This time, however, the ageing Waterford side were coming to the end of their glory years. Not surprisingly, Eddie ran riot, scoring 14 points, 10 from frees. He had already scored 2–5 in the Leinster semi-final. Although already a star by reputation, this was one of the early televised finals on Telefís Éireann and it demonstrated Eddie's outstanding scoring talents on the national stage. For the record, Kilkenny beat Waterford by 4–17 to 6–8.

'I think that Waterford team, in the late 1950s and early '60s, was one of the best teams ever,' Eddie says. 'They played a tremendous brand of hurling. They were ahead of their time in the way they played the game. In the modern era they would have been unbeatable, I think. But, that being so, they were coming towards the end of that team in '63 and we were coming with a new team.

'I remember about two weeks before the game I just couldn't get my free-taking right. I was in Dublin at the time and we trained up in Terenure College. Martin Walsh, who played with me in St Kieran's College, and I went out to practise. I said: "Martin, I can't get these frees right!" "Remember," he said, "what did Tommy Maher tell you?" I thought back to Kieran's College and I worked on it and suddenly things were happening.

'Things were on fire for me in the final in '63. I got ten frees, I think, and I scored ten of them. I got 14 points in all. Either in the frees or any time I put my hurley to the ball, it just came right for me. When I ran into position, it just came right for me. There were other days as well where things happened like that. It's an amazing feeling: the ball is there, you can go into positions, suddenly the ball is coming to you, you put your hurl to it and suddenly it's in your hand.

'I had plenty of the other days as well where, no matter what you did, you were either in the wrong place and the ball was gone inside you, or when you did get a chance you fluffed the ball and you weren't able to control it. It's hard to explain those days. I don't know whether it's mental or physical, I'm not sure.

'I think it's being tuned in. People say after matches: "Ah, sure, the ball ran for him." Or they say: "No matter where the team was, the ball broke for him." I firmly believe that's due to your mental approach. I think the greatest gift in playing hurling is to read the game and to be able to judge your team-mates, to be able to know that you have to work that split second before the fellow marking you. If you can read the game, where the ball is going to come from based on your knowledge of your team-mates, then you have the advantage.

'That's the only way as a forward you can get an advantage over a back. In play, the back has all the advantages. The forward has to get one step ahead of him or work out some things to beat him because the back really only has to beat back the ball or hit it back up the field. A forward has to get the ball and has to round or get around or hit backwards to either score or hit the ball to a colleague. The point I'm making is that the reading of the game, and being able to read the game, is probably the single biggest asset you could have as a hurler.'

In the 1970s Kilkenny became by far the most powerful and dominant force in the game of hurling. Back in 1967 they had beaten an ageing Tipperary team, securing All-Ireland medal number two for Eddie Keher. Two years later they repeated the achievement, this time defeating Cork with Eddie as captain. But now, in the 1970s, a well-balanced Kilkenny side combining tight defence with a strong midfield and some devastating forward play threatened to take over the game.

In the five years from 1971 to 1975 Kilkenny never missed an All-Ireland final at Croke Park. Along the way, up to 1979, they won four All-Ireland finals. Eddie shared in three of those successes. With the exception of the Rebel County, few teams could live with the Kilkenny side of the 1970s.

'Father Maher was working on the team ever since the time he took over with Kilkenny,' Eddie recalls. 'I'd say he felt, at that stage in the '70s, that he had developed what he regarded as the perfect team. He had strength where it was needed and skill where it was needed, and he was able to develop a certain pattern of team play that worked for us and that we were good at playing as a team.

'Father Maher was, as I said, very much ahead of his time in coaching methods. I mean, his coaching methods are still being used by coaches now. He was the first, with Donie Nealon and Des Ferguson, to actually set down on paper coaching methods and coaching exercises and to develop a style of play that was designed to win games rather than look good. In the early '60s Kilkenny were always regarded as being a light team, sort of stylish, maybe easily put off. But over the '60s Kilkenny got a few very strong players, particularly down the middle, and by the time the decade was over they were able to hold their own with any team.

'It probably was beginning to take shape in '69. Then we contested the '71, '72, '73, '74 and '75 All-Ireland finals. We had five All-Ireland finals in that period. Also, I suppose that team backboned the Leinster team of that era, which had a tremendous five-in-a-row run over Munster. That was sort of unheard of. It was a great team and probably will go down as one of the great teams of any era, I'd say. The more we won, the more we wanted to win. We developed great team spirit that time.

'We were very fortunate, also, that the period was the beginning of the first All-Stars. The All-Ireland winners and the All-Star team got trips to the west coast of America, which was really a dream come true for everyone in the '70s. We had gone to New York and Chicago and places on the east coast of America but to go to the west coast was absolutely unbelievable. We had tremendous trips there, which also served to bond that particular team together.

'I don't ever remember that team getting tired of winning. Every match they went out to play, they wanted to win. They worked hard for one another and they got a great attitude going. If there was any sign of laziness or any sign of over-confidence or anything coming into the team there were always fellows on the team to stand up and make sure everyone got their act together. No matter what game we were playing, whether it was in San Francisco or whether it was in New York or whether it was in a challenge game opening a field in Waterford or Tipperary or wherever, the team wanted to win.'

Eddie Keher's 1970s All-Ireland medals were won in 1972 against Cork, in 1974 against Limerick and in 1975 against Galway. The classic was the 1972 final against Cork, in which Eddie scored two memorable goals. The 1974 final was a tightly contested affair until Kilkenny's victory was secured in the second half, helped on by Eddie's tally of 1–11. The following year Eddie won his sixth All-Ireland senior medal while scoring 2–7 in his team's defeat of Galway.

By now Eddie was in his mid-thirties and he had achieved all the great honours of the game. He had won five consecutive All-Stars. He was voted Hurler of the Year in 1972. He had won three National Hurling League titles to add to his six All-Ireland medals. Success at that level requires extraordinary dedication and commitment and by 1977 the hard graft and the wear and tear had taken their toll. In November 1977, some 21 years since he first wore the black and amber as a Kilkenny minor, Eddie Keher retired.

'The first thing I'd say I noticed in myself was that my burst of speed was going,' Eddie remarks. 'I think it was in the 1977 Leinster final, where we were beaten by Wexford. We were two or three points down coming into the last minute and I managed to get a ball about 35 yards out. I made for a goal and normally in that position I wouldn't be caught for speed. But I couldn't shake off the Wexford backs. I only got a half-shot at goal, which I think was touched over the crossbar by the keeper for a point. The first feeling I had was that I knew I wasn't able to hit fast on the run: that my legs were beginning to slow down.

'Then up to the period that I actually retired, which was in 1977, we were contesting the championship here. I remember we had been beaten in a couple of county finals and were struggling hard to try and win another county championship. We had two draws and a win and then we were in the county final. We were beaten in the county final. Kilkenny were playing the following Sunday and I suddenly felt, for the first time in my life, that I was just drained of energy. I felt for the first time ever that I'm not going to be able to play another game. I told the selectors that I was going to give it up. It just came about like that, it wasn't any long-term planning or anything.'

By the time he retired Eddie Keher had laid claim to the title of being the deadliest finisher in the history of hurling. Year after year he topped the scoring charts, delivering century-plus scores season by season. In his day he demolished all previous scoring records, especially the highest individual score in an All-Ireland final. He was also responsible for the highest score ever in a season, with a total of 20–134, or 194 points, scored in 1972.

It wasn't, however, just the records that established Eddie Keher's hurling pedigree. Above all, Eddie was a player with flair, intelligence and imagination, capable of producing remarkable scores and memorable moments. He was a prototype of the polished striker, who delivered some of his finest performances in crucial matches, especially in the heat of All-Ireland finals. He also had an insight into the game only seen in those who study it carefully. Having spanned the decades from the late 1950s to the late '70s, he was an automatic choice on the Team of the Millennium.

'I saw a lot of changes in style in the game which teams had to adapt to as they went along,' Eddie concludes. 'The great Wexford team of the '50s had brought in the catching of the ball in a forest of hurleys, so to speak, which was a tremendous skill and which changed the pattern of games. Other people had to adapt to it. Other changes took place in the '60s with the great Tipperary teams. They introduced another lot of skills like the backs batting forward the ball and not allowing a double on the ball. We had to adapt to that as well and try and introduce tactics that would counteract all these new skills.

'Then you had the '70s rule changes. I played through all those. I found, as I went on, that the new rules and the new skills that were being developed also helped my game because they suited my game. I was very fortunate to come in the era I did. I got the end of, we'll say, the '50s team. I was fortunate that the great team of the '60s was there, that I was lucky enough to play with them, which developed in to the great team of the '70s. I have great memories of all those teams, all those players and all those games.

'I think flair and style, to my mind, are up there at the top of hurling. There have been many rule changes made in the last number of years which I think, in some ways, have been designed to curb individual flair. But despite all that, it hasn't detracted from the game mainly because the players were able to overcome the rule changes that were made by introducing new skills.

'Individual flair is part and parcel of Gaelic games and particularly hurling, and if that is ever taken out of the game I think it will ruin the game. As long as All-Irelands are won and teams are great because they have that individual as well as collective flair, and as long as style still wins over robust tactics, then I think the game will live forever and will always be as great as it is now.'

12. TONY DORAN

THE SCORING CAREER OF WEXFORD SHARPSHOOTER TONY DORAN HAD AN INAUSPICIOUS beginning. The occasion was Tony's first-ever game in the local Nicky Rackard Schools League. It took place back in the 1950s, when Tony was little more than ten years of age. His father was there, other parents were there, mentors were there and, of course, a pitch-full of young hurlers had togged out for the game.

It must have been an omen for the future when Tony was slotted in as a forward, having come on as a substitute. As so often happens in under-age hurling, for a long time he didn't get a touch of the ball. Then, in an instant, the ball came his way and history was made as the future Wexford legend took his first strike in competitive hurling.

Tony laughs at the memory, as vivid now as it was back in the 1950s. 'It was my first game in the Rackard League,' he recalls. 'I think I was ten at the time. At that time the schools league was U-14, so I was only a small little boy among all these fellows. I came on as sub at half-time and I was playing corner-forward.

'Eventually, the ball came somewhere within a few yards of the end line. I could have been halfway between the goal and the sideline. I was facing away from the goal. I just pulled in the direction I was facing. It went straight out over the end line. I thought I was doing great work to get a stroke of the ball, even though I wasn't hitting it in the right direction. It was probably the first and only stroke I got.

'The match was in an ordinary farmer's field, where they used to play matches at that time, in a place called Mount Daniel. There would have been a good few people there. I recall it was sort of a wet and damp old evening. I remember it a lot better than I even remember All-Irelands. It's just something that stuck in my mind. I got told off on the way home in the car. My dad said: "You don't do those things." I never forgot it and I never did it again, anyhow.'

Born near Boolavogue, Tony Doran grew up steeped in the history of his native county. The surrounding land evoked memories of Father John Murphy and the rebel pikemen of 1798. By the 1950s, however, those legendary pikemen were being superseded by new heroes from the Wexford hurling team. As if from nowhere, great hurlers like Nicky, Bobby and Billy Rackard, Ned Wheeler, Padge Kehoe and Nick O'Donnell burst on the scene. By the mid-1950s they were contesting three All-Ireland finals, setting Wexford alight with two dramatic victories in 1955 and '56.

'I would barely remember when they started to get prominent in the early '50s,' Tony says. 'I would have been about eight, nine and ten when they went to the three All-Irelands in a row from 1954 to 1956 and, you know, I wasn't at any of them. The first time I was in Croke Park was in 1955. I was at the All-Ireland semi-final when Wexford played Limerick. I don't remember a lot about it, only being up on the top of the Cusack Stand, nearly at the very back, and seeing all those fellows like the Rackards, Padge Kehoe and Ned Wheeler. But at the time I suppose the idol for everyone growing up in Wexford was Nicky Rackard.

'At that time Nicky had started up the Rackard League, a competition for schools in Wexford. There was no competition in schools at the time, nothing except for the league started up by Nicky in the mid-'50s. I remember on one occasion that we played, Nicky was actually the referee. I think it was a quarter-final or something like that. That was a very big occasion, of course, for all the lads playing. I suppose they all wanted to be Nicky Rackard. When you were out playing games in the evenings, or after school, everyone wanted to be Nicky Rackard. Little did you think that maybe you would be in the same position a few years later.'

The path to Wexford's All-Ireland success in the late 1960s can be tracked, at least partly, through the earlier triumphs of the county's minor and U-21 sides. Predictably, the same path marks the progress of Tony Doran from promising young hurler to All-Ireland winner. Back in 1963 the Wexford minors, with Tony on board, beat Limerick in the All-Ireland minor final. Two years later half a dozen of those minors, including Tony, achieved U-21 championship honours by defeating Tipperary in the All-Ireland U-21 final.

In turn, by 1968 half a dozen of the U-21s had progressed to a senior championship triumph, again with Tony Doran operating as one of the stars of the side. Within five years the bones of a new Wexford senior team had been built from the bottom up. At the core of that team was Tony Doran: the powerful and accomplished forward, strongly built, with a fearless temperament and a devastating ability to score.

'I never seemed to play anywhere else, only in the forwards,' Tony recalls. 'I played around midfield as well, at under-age level, but I can never recall having played in the backs at all. I always seemed to be playing from midfield up. From the time I came on as a corner-forward in the Nicky Rackard League with the Boolavogue school team, I always seemed to stay at that end of the field.

'You got used to playing in the forwards. You had to use your head a certain amount to try and create openings to get scores or lay off the ball. You got used to scoring. Maybe it didn't always happen. But the one thing on your mind, every time a ball came, was that you should try and get a score. The majority of times you thought you'd get a goal. It didn't always happen but I think it developed naturally in that way.'

He was always described by Micheál O'Hehir as 'the red-haired Tony Doran from Boolavogue' and nowhere was that description more in use than in Tony's great career highlight, the 1968 All-Ireland final against Tipperary. For Wexford, certainly there were scores to settle. Back in 1962 and '65 the great Jimmy Doyle had captained his county to All-Ireland victories over Wexford. But now, in 1968, Tipperary were fading and a fresh, enthusiastic Wexford side, with their flame-haired sharpshooter Tony Doran, were waiting in ambush.

Few All-Ireland finals could match the drama and excitement of the 1968 contest. In the early exchanges Tony Doran was closely marked by Mick Roche. At half-time, eight points down, things looked bleak for Wexford. It was a game of contrasting halves, however, with Tony's two crucial goals in the second period reviving Wexford's fortunes. In one of the great reversals in All-Ireland hurling history, Wexford went eight points ahead and ended up victors by a score of 5–8 to 3–12.

'We went into the 1968 final probably as underdogs,' Tony says. 'We had been there or thereabouts for a couple of years before but we were underdogs going in against what was sort of the remains of a great Tipperary team of the early '60s. On that occasion we were playing in both senior and minor finals. That was the first time it had ever happened in Wexford. To come away with a win in both games is still looked back on as a very big occasion.

'In the first half it was very much one-way traffic and at half-time we looked to be dead and buried. We got our act together after half-time. We got a few scores, got back in the game and from there on, for the last 20 minutes, it was a see-saw effort as we hauled back the Tipperary lead. We went in front ourselves and Tipperary hauled us back. Then coming near the end we were hanging on to win by two points. It's hard to recall how you felt during it because you hadn't really the time to think how you were feeling. There seemed to be so much happening on the day.

'Strangely enough, I don't remember all that much about the homecoming. I remember at that time we were travelling by car. A few fellows from the different localities would all be travelling together. I know that, in our case, we had a couple of us travelling that were on the senior panel and a couple off the minor panel. I can remember big crowds in the first stop, Gorey, but as the journey home went on it's a little bit more vague in my mind. But it was a great event. It's the only time that I experienced anything like it.'

In subsequent years, up to the mid-1970s, Wexford's All-Ireland title ambitions were thwarted largely by the rise of Kilkenny. Despite Wexford's success in 1968, they struggled, year after year, to emerge from Leinster against one of the finest sides in hurling history. They did break Kilkenny's stranglehold in 1970, winning the Leinster title. However, having beaten Galway in the All-Ireland semi-final, Wexford tasted defeat against Cork in the championship decider.

For the next five years the annual Leinster finals between Wexford and Kilkenny were tense affairs, some closer than others. In all those years Wexford went home disappointed. Most frustrating were the tight contests, such as 1974, when a point scored by Eddie Keher in the dying seconds secured the narrowest of victories for the Noresiders. Following that defeat it was tough for Wexford to watch the Leinster champions stroll to All-Ireland victory with easy wins over Galway and Limerick.

'Particularly in the '70s, there was a great rivalry between ourselves and Kilkenny,' Tony says. 'From our point of view we always seemed to come out on the wrong side of it. The Kilkenny team of the first half of the '70s, I suppose, was one of the best teams ever. We used to meet them every year in the Leinster final and for five years in a row, from '71 to '75, they beat us. In that period they went on to win three All-Irelands.

'The fact that we were a close second-best to them in Leinster maybe was nice in one way but at the same time it didn't bring us a lot of joy. It meant that we had to make an extra effort, in the '70s, to finally lay the Kilkenny bogey and get out of Leinster. Eventually, it happened in '76 when we went to Croke Park as underdogs and beat them by something like 17 points. It will always stand out as a great occasion for us to finally get the better of Kilkenny after so many heartbreaks.'

Kilkenny's stranglehold over Wexford was broken in 1976 with the Slaneysiders recording a stunning Leinster final victory by a score of 2–20 to 1–6. Escaping at last from their province, Wexford narrowly squeezed past Galway in the All-Ireland semi-final and faced Cork in the September decider. Despite a crucial goal by Tony Doran, it was the Cork side, captained by Ray Cummins, which powered its way to victory.

The following year brought a replay of the 1976 All-Ireland, with Cork and Wexford again battling for honours. In the Leinster final Wexford once more defeated Kilkenny, winning their second Leinster title in a row. Having sprung the Leinster trap, however, they failed to sparkle in September and lost to a Cork side that were now in phase two of a historic three-in-a-row. The disappointment in Wexford was crushing. Having grafted for so long to overcome Kilkenny, all they achieved was a brace of All-Ireland defeats.

'In 1976 we felt we had played well on the day but maybe we missed a couple of chances,' Tony recalls. 'We gave away a few scores that maybe we should have prevented. It's all about preventing scores and taking scores. That's what Cork did and they got there. They got a couple of chances in the end and they won by three or four points. We had a chance, nearly on full-time, when we felt we should have got a free in. I was involved in it myself. We didn't get it and we just had to move on. If we had got it, maybe we would have got a goal, maybe we wouldn't. But as it was, we couldn't deny Cork their victory.

'In 1977 I think there was no doubt that Cork were the better team. We didn't play to our potential on the day. Cork were in command nearly the whole game, yet we could have snatched it in the end. We had got back within three points and Christy Keogh had a shot that brought a great save from Martin Coleman just seconds from the end. It was sort of strange, in a way. We played well in '76 and Cork pipped us. We played badly in '77 and nearly went closer to winning than we did in '76.

'We were probably very unlucky to run up against a Cork team that, in that period, went and won three in a row. I think the Cork team at that time weren't given credit for being the team they were. I think they were a very good Cork team, even though a lot of people didn't think it at the time. When you look back on it and look at the names that were in it, they would have to be regarded as one of the finest teams of my period, anyhow.

'OK, it probably was getting a bit frustrating that, for so many years, Kilkenny were pipping us by the odd point, or two or three points, in Leinster finals and they were going on to win All-Irelands. Finally, when we beat Kilkenny in two Leinster finals in a row, Cork came and pipped us. It was a bit frustrating but that's how it goes and you have to put up with those things. I suppose it's a great honour to play in an All-Ireland final. But really, when the All-Ireland final is over, no matter what happens there are winners and losers. It's the same right down along the line to a club game and a county final. There are winners and losers, and it's winners take all.'

While the formidable presence of Kilkenny undoubtedly restricted Tony Doran's All-Ireland ambitions in the 1970s, the Noresiders ironically helped contribute to some of his most notable successes. It would be hard to conjure a team of greater quality than one containing the likes of Kilkenny's Eddie Keher, Frank Cummins, Noel Skehan and Pat Henderson, along with Mick Jacob, Tony Doran and Martin Quigley of Wexford. But that's exactly the calibre of player that powered Leinster, and Tony Doran, to five Railway Cups in a row, from 1971 to 1975, adding a further two in 1977 and 1979.

'We had a strong squad at all times,' Tony says of those Leinster teams. 'The majority of the players on all occasions were either Kilkenny or Wexford and I think that the success at the time reflected the strength of hurling in both counties. The fact that Wexford and Kilkenny always seemed to blend pretty well together in those games had a big bearing on our success at the time.'

Tony also experienced success at club level, winning the All-Ireland championship in 1989 with his club, Buffers Alley. A small club with a tiny hinterland, Buffers Alley defied hurling logic with a long sequence of county championship victories. They also courted All-Ireland club success, although it took until 1989, when they beat Antrim's O'Donovan Rossa, for Buffers Alley to finally achieve their All-Ireland goal. At that stage Tony was very much in the twilight of his hurling career. His inter-county career was over and his final days as a club hurler were about to come to a close.

'I'd say success with Buffers Alley probably meant more to me in hurling than anything else ever meant,' Tony reflects. 'When I was growing up, we were just a struggling junior club. I came into it at a time when we were starting to achieve success and getting into senior ranks. We were beaten in the All-Ireland final in March 1986. We felt that maybe, at the time, we had missed our chance of All-Ireland success. But we came back three years later and we won our All-Ireland title and, to me, that was really a great occasion. I'd say it was the greatest occasion I've had in hurling, to win at local level with all your own all around you.

'But everything finally comes to an end. I never retired from inter-county. I never retired from club. I just stopped being part of it. My last game in inter-county was the 1984 Leinster final against Offaly. Offaly beat us by a point in the centenary year and I just drifted out of it after that. I kept playing on with the club until I finally finished up at the beginning of '93, I think it was, after a county junior hurling final. I was a grade back at that stage and we were beaten by a point. That was the last game that I played.'

Throughout his career Tony Doran won many awards, most notably Hurler of the Year in 1976. He also won one All-Star award and two National Hurling League titles to add to his single senior All-Ireland won in 1968. But for Cork in 1970, '76 and '77, Tony might have added to his All-Ireland collection; and but for Kilkenny in the 1970s, he might have made it to more of the penultimate and ultimate stages of the hurling championship. But it was not to be.

As it was, Tony Doran stood out in his county's campaigns as one of the game's great forwards and he showed in Railway Cup contests that he could match the best from Munster while settling in with ease alongside his Kilkenny counterparts in the Leinster side. Above all, he helped fashion one of Wexford's greatest eras, appearing in four All-Ireland finals. In doing so, he helped bridge the gap between Wexford's successes of the 1950s and the county's later All-Ireland triumph in 1996.

'Having the likes of Wexford to the forefront is very important to the GAA,' Tony concludes. 'The joy it brought to Wexford in '96 was something else. It was great to experience it, to witness it, even though I went through it myself nearly 30 years before. I think in '96 it really brought home to me what it meant to the people of Wexford to win an All-Ireland. When you were on the outside yourself, it was much easier to see it than when you were part of it while playing.

'I have great memories. There was a time back in the 1968 All-Ireland when, after Wexford fought back, the teams had been level for maybe six or eight minutes without any score. I was lucky enough to get a ball, get inside my man and get a goal that put us in front with less than ten minutes left. The likes of that would stick in your memory.

'On another occasion we played Kilkenny in a Leinster semi-final in my last year, 1984, and we were again in the same position. We were level coming in to the last couple of minutes and the game was see-sawing. Billy Byrne, who was playing midfield for Wexford, hit a high ball and I happened to catch it in front of Dick O'Hara. I got around him and put it in the net. It was the decisive score. Little things like that would stand out.

'I had very good times. I was lucky. I lasted for a good few years and escaped serious injury. I couldn't have any complaints. OK, we didn't win All-Irelands but we were one of the teams that were reckoned to be in with a chance of success. It mightn't have happened but at the same time we were always there or thereabouts. We were always in the thick of it.'

13. NOEL SKEHAN

FOR A GOALKEEPER TO MAKE THE SAME MISTAKE TWICE IS LITTLE SHORT OF A CRIME.
Once is regrettable, twice unforgivable. Such was the motto put into
practice by Kilkenny's Noel Skehan early on in his hurling life. The
year was 1961. There was, as yet, no Croke Park appearance, no sign
of the record nine All-Ireland medals or seven All-Star awards that, in
time, would come his way. In fact, Noel was still honing his skills with
his native Bennettsbridge, hoping and waiting for a break with the
Kilkenny minors.

'In 1961 I was playing for the Bennettsbridge minors when I was
told I was to go to Kilkenny for a trial,' Noel recalls. 'There was a trial
on the next Sunday in Nowlan Park. I got this card stating I was picked
for a trial and that a car would call for me at a particular time. I was
sitting at home, waiting on this car to call for me and no car called.
There was no trial, no nothing.

'Kilkenny went on and won the All-Ireland that year in 1961. Then
at the start of '62 I had an idea that I'd be in the running again for a
place on the minor team. I had a bit of a chance, anyway, of making it
because I was playing with the Bennettsbridge junior team, which was
a pretty good team. Bennettsbridge were very, very strong at the time.

'Anyway, this card arrived stating the same thing: a trial at Nowlan
Park at such a time and a car will call for you. I didn't gamble on the
car calling for me. Instead, I got up on my bicycle and I was there an
hour before the trial. I got the trial and I made the team. That was the
last time I waited on a car to call for me, as far as the minors were
concerned anyway.'

No player in hurling history has matched the astonishing record of
nine All-Ireland medals won by Noel Skehan from 1963 to 1983. With

three of those medals won as substitute, his record is surpassed by the eight All-Irelands of both Christy Ring and John Doyle, which were won as full team members on the field of play. By their sheer volume, however, Noel's haul of All-Ireland trophies is testimony both to Kilkenny's prominence in hurling over those decades and his own remarkable pedigree as a legend between the Kilkenny posts.

Born in Bennettsbridge, one of the hotbeds of Kilkenny hurling, it would have been hard for Noel Skehan to escape his destiny as a hurler. His uncle, Dan Kennedy, captained Kilkenny to a famous All-Ireland triumph in 1947, leading his team to victory over Cork in one of the most thrilling finals ever seen at Croke Park. Noel's mother was also first cousin to the great Kilkenny goalkeeper Ollie Walsh, who would soon play a central role in the development of her son's inter-county career. However, it was in the immediate surroundings of the family home in Bennettsbridge that the young Noel Skehan's interest in hurling first blossomed.

'My first pair of boots came from England, from another uncle called Paddy Kennedy,' Noel recollects. 'I was on to him all the time to send me home a pair of boots. He sent me home a pair of brown hurling boots and I definitely thought it was my birthday, I can tell you that. I can still see them vividly. The boots were lovely. I wore them the first day and I didn't even want to dirty them. I brought them home and I remember there were a few marks on them and I was asking how I would get the marks off them. I was annoyed that the boots were even marked.

'I remember the first hurl as well. It came from a shop in Parliament Street in Kilkenny. That same shop, Liam Moore's, is there now but they don't sell hurls or anything like that. But I remember getting this new hurl brought home to me with whatever name he used to have on it, Liam Moore or whatever. Even at that time, when you'd go out hurling and when you'd dirty it, you'd come home and start cleaning the hurl. You wouldn't want to be hurling on a wet day or a bad day or anything like that, when you'd have to clean it up.

'The Ring was the name of where I lived and there was a guy, Lord have mercy on him, Paddy Kelly was his name, who lived beside me. The houses were joined on to one another. I used to be out in the back beating this ball at dinner times, evenings, every minute and hour, every chance that I got. I can always remember one occasion when

Paddy Kelly, who used to work in the creamery, was up for his dinner. There was a dividing wall between the two houses and I missed the wall. The ball went flying through the window and Paddy was having his dinner. I got an awful fright. But all he said was: "Once you play for Kilkenny, I'll be happy." But I missed the wall a fair few times and I broke more windows and panes of glass on that man, 'twas unreal.

'There was nothing else to do around here at that stage. You had a hurl, you were lucky to have a ball, you had a hurling pitch and you were out watching the senior team training, watching them playing matches. Your only interest at that stage was hurling. You lived for it, you died for it, and you'd do anything to wear the green and gold of Bennettsbridge or the black and amber of Kilkenny. I trained, I'd say, every day of the week. I always had a hurley in my hand. They tell me that there's something like 125 skills in hurling, left and right and all the different sides. To be honest about it, to get a third of them right you'd have to have a hurl pretty often in your hand.'

Noel Skehan's rise through the Kilkenny ranks was nothing short of meteoric. Having joined up with the minors in 1962, he played in goal for their All-Ireland-winning side that year and won many admirers in the process. With his goalkeeper cousin Ollie Walsh firmly established in the senior side, the Skehan and Walsh clans had copper-fastened their grip on two of the county's major net-minding positions. Ironically, by the following year Noel was elevated to the senior panel and both cousins, together, were on their way to senior All-Ireland success at Croke Park.

Throughout the decade of the 1960s the parade of the Walsh and Skehan cousins to Croke Park became something of an annual ritual. For the rest of that decade alone Kilkenny reached five All-Ireland finals, winning three. Along the way they beat Waterford in 1963, Tipperary in 1967 and Cork in 1969. They also lost to Cork and Tipperary. Except for a period in the mid-1960s when he was injured, Noel Skehan sat on the bench while his second cousin Ollie Walsh played in goal.

'In 1963 I was only coming on to the Bennettsbridge senior team when I was picked for the Kilkenny senior team as well. I was surprised. I couldn't believe it. I was being told that I was to go in training with the senior team and to go in then and be a sub. It was a big thing for me, just coming out of the minor ranks, especially being a sub to Ollie.

'To me and to everyone else at the time, Ollie was definitely the best keeper around. He was a big man, far bigger than me, and able to deal with high shots a lot different than I had to deal with them. I had to kind of negotiate my own ways of dealing with high balls. But I was watching him for a long time and I learned a lot from him.

'He was a super keeper in his own way. He had brilliant ways of dealing with shots, let them be high, let them be low, let them be whatever way you like. He was very fast and he was very helpful to me arriving in there as a young lad. Anything could happen, you could be called in at any stage. Going in there and being a sub to the best keeper in Ireland wasn't easy but I suppose it was easier being a sub than trying to replace him. I was the bones of ten years looking at him and I served my time.

'People used to say to me: "How do you continue going there and you only a sub all the time?" But I didn't look at it that way. Kilkenny had a super team in the '60s and it was an honour for me to be a sub to a giant like Ollie Walsh. I won three All-Irelands and I think a lot of the three medals. Everyone is still talking about the three as a sub but to me I don't give a damn. Definitely, in the '60s, there was no better keeper around and Kilkenny were very strong at the time.

'I was quite happy to be a sub. Maybe that's the wrong thing to say. You should never be happy to be a sub because you're always trying to win your place on the team. But to win your place on the team against such a very good goalkeeper as Ollie wasn't a simple thing. I knew I had to stay there a certain length of time to try and get my place. That's the way I looked at it and I worked hard at it.'

If the decade of the 1960s belonged to Ollie Walsh, then the 1970s saw the tables dramatically turned as Noel Skehan took over in the Kilkenny goal. Seven times that decade Kilkenny travelled to Croke Park to contest All-Ireland finals and four times they won. In the first, in 1971, they lost to Tipperary, with the veteran Ollie Walsh still in goal. From then on, however, the goalkeeper's jersey belonged to Noel Skehan and he grabbed his chance with some style.

'The first time I was picked was in a league game, after Kilkenny got beaten by Tipperary in the 1971 All-Ireland final,' Noel recalls. 'Ollie was a sub that day to me. It was funny, really, to be quite honest. It was no big deal for him. He said to me: "Make it your own, now." I suppose the easiest thing for Ollie to do at that time was to have bowed out and gone away from the scene. But he didn't. He stayed, fair dues to him.

He stayed there for all of 1971 and into '72, as a sub. That was a great honour for me, to have such a keeper there as understudy to me.

'The first game wasn't easy. I knew in my heart and soul, coming into the Kilkenny team at that stage, that "unless you're going to play brilliant, boy, you're going to be in trouble". Everyone will be saying "You're not as good as Ollie" and all the rest. I knew too that I wasn't going to make it in a day or a year. This was going to take a bit of time. You don't fill Ollie Walsh's boots in a day or a year and anyone thinking that is crazy. But after hanging in for the bones of ten years, it would have been stupid to let it slip.

'When you're not playing, and when you're a sub, you get the odd league or Oireachtas game and things like that. But you don't really know how you're going to perform until you get in there and you're left there for a while. The big thing is to get confidence in the things you do yourself and the way you do them. I had picked up an awful lot from sitting on the sideline for so long watching Ollie. But to get out and do it was another thing. You need the confidence you get from playing matches and playing behind the same type of backs and getting used to them.

'No matter what shot, whether it's a high shot, low shot, whatever shot it is, you had to have the confidence to think that you were going to save it. No matter where a forward was, you thought you'd stop it, be it 10 yards, 15 yards or 40 yards. But I would say that confidence was a thing I got, more than anything else, from watching Ollie and from beginning to play the matches in the '70s and up along. It came from getting used to doing things over and over and over again and getting used to playing behind the backs and all of that.'

Throughout the 1970s Kilkenny and Cork shared the hurling headlines, winning four All-Irelands each. Not to be outdone by Cork's 1970 victory and their subsequent three-in-a-row from 1976 to 1978, Kilkenny grabbed their own share of the spoils. They won in 1972, with Noel Skehan as captain, and they won again in 1974, '75 and '79. Very few teams could match the power and style of the Kilkenny team that emerged in that era.

With Skehan in goal Kilkenny boasted a last line of defence that was the envy of all other counties. He repeatedly defied opposing attackers with his confidence, his agility, his reflexes and his command of the Kilkenny back line. He negated some of the finest hurlers of his generation, especially from Cork, Galway and from fellow-Leinster opponents, Wexford. Few goalkeepers broke as many opposing supporters' hearts as Kilkenny's Noel Skehan.

'It was fantastic in 1972 because the previous year we won the championship here in Bennettsbridge and the club made me captain. Here I was, in my first year playing for this Kilkenny team, and I found myself captain. But the captain part didn't worry me a lot because after tossing the coin I didn't put any emphasis on speeches or anything else. They were far away in the back of my head.

'Anyway, we found ourselves in an All-Ireland final against Cork and a hell of a good Cork team it was too. The forwards they had, they'd frighten you. We were lucky enough to win it. I can remember we were eight points down and I can still see Con Roche hitting the ball over the bar from under the Cusack Stand. I don't know if that was the seventh or eighth point they went ahead by. I thought: "This looks like it is gone from us." But, fair dues to the boys, they kept at it. We got going and Eddie Keher and Frank Cummins got goals. It was super to win it and it was super to be captain of a great team. To beat Cork in an All-Ireland final is really brilliant and to be captain makes it that much better.

'However, I would say that the 1973 team was possibly the best team I played on. We didn't win the All-Ireland. We were short of players. Three or four players went on us after the Leinster final that year. That Leinster final win against Wexford was as good a performance as I've ever seen out of a Kilkenny team. The display by Kilkenny was really super. I don't want to take anything from Limerick, they won the All-Ireland and that's it, end of story. But we were short of some very good players. In '74 we got our revenge.

'Kilkenny had good players at that time. Every one in the team in the '70s was great, powerful, and you had backbone. The backs were super. I needn't tell you about the forwards, the likes of Eddie Keher, to name but one, and Mick Crotty, Mick Brennan, Pat Delaney, Kieran Purcell. I can go on forever. You had to take a hell of a battling to stop those forwards. You might stop Eddie Keher today but then you'd have the likes of Pat Delaney or Kieran Purcell coming up trumps. Stop Purcell or Delaney the next day and you'd have Crotty or Brennan or Billy Fitzpatrick coming up trumps.

'They were a really good team. People will tell you that we should have won another All-Ireland or two but I suppose in Kilkenny we think we have a divine right to win the All-Ireland every year. I suppose they think the same in Cork and Tipperary and everywhere else. But that's the way you must think and that's the way you should think. It was a great time for Kilkenny. It was a great time for me, in particular, for the simple reason that I was lucky enough to be around at a time when Kilkenny won so many All-Irelands.'

By the end of the 1970s Noel Skehan had amassed seven All-Ireland medals, four from the field of play and three won as substitute in the 1960s. He was, by then, a multiple All-Star award-winner and he had built up a reputation as one of the finest goalkeepers the game had ever produced. Memories of Ollie Walsh had long receded in the consciousness of Kilkenny supporters.

With typical confidence, Noel and his Kilkenny colleagues marched into the 1980s in search of more hurling glory. In time, that confidence bore fruit. In 1982 and '83 they broke Cork captain Jimmy Barry-Murphy's heart with two convincing All-Ireland final defeats. Noel Skehan's All-Ireland medal collection, already weighty, now jumped to nine. In one of those finals, in 1982, a curious event occurred involving an apple.

'I'll tell you what happened about the apple,' Noel says with a smile. 'In 1982 there was about a minute left in the game, something like that, and the ball went wide. We were a few points up, we were pretty safe at the time. I went back behind the goal to get the ball and there was no sign of it coming. The next thing, this "thing" arrives in, which I thought was the ball. I put out my hand for it and caught it. I saw that it was an apple and a hell of a nice-looking apple it was too.

'I was thinking of throwing it back but I didn't. I just brought the apple into the goal and left it down beside the goalpost. Noel O'Donoghue was the referee at the time and the crowd were beginning to come in on the field. Noel O'Donoghue said to me: "Noel, hit out that ball or I'll call the match off." "Well, Noel," I said, "I've no ball to hit out, I've only an apple." He looked and he said: "Yeah, it's only an apple."

'Eventually, we got a ball to hit out. I struck it out and the game was over in about a minute or so. I collected my two other hurls in the back of the net and collected the apple as well. I rubbed it and I thought it looked a hell of a nice apple. I was kind of hungry at the time, so I started eating the apple. I was eating it going along. Eventually, I got up to the Hogan Stand and Joe Hennessy was beside me. The next thing, he said: "Where did you get that apple?" I just said: "I got it." He took it off me and started eating it as well.

'I'd say everyone in Kilkenny that I've spoken to at this stage, they've thrown the apple in. They say, more or less: "Did you like the apple I threw in to you?" Everyone – north, south, east and west – they all threw it in. I don't know who threw it in, to be quite honest with you. But it was a nice apple, I can tell you, after winning an All-Ireland in '82.'

Noel Skehan finally retired as Kilkenny goalkeeper in 1985, having won seven All-Star awards and accumulated a historic nine All-Ireland senior medals. He won 11 Leinster titles, along with a haul of National Hurling League, Oireachtas and Railway Cup medals together with Save of the Year and Man of the Match awards. He also received a coveted Texaco Hurler of the Year award in 1982. Few other exponents of the game could match that volume of career achievements. Even less could come close to his longevity in some of the finest teams in hurling history.

'I went from 1963 to 1985, really. It's a long time,' Noel concludes. 'I played a lot of matches, made a lot of friends. I played against a lot of great forwards, the best of forwards from every county. There was great enjoyment in it. There was a big lot of work in it, a big lot of effort, a mighty lot of training put in. The older you get, the harder you must train. Experience won't get you the ball that's 15 yards away. Experience is useful when you have the ball but the big thing is to get the ball.

'I had to train very, very hard in those years, running, playing badminton, anything at all just to keep me fit. When I got a bit older I started playing squash. I started to play squash to keep my eye keen, to keep my fitness level up. In hindsight now, when I think about it, it was brilliant. It was great to be part of the scene. Kilkenny had great teams in that era and I was bloody lucky to be on them.

'I didn't put too much emphasis on six, seven, eight or nine medals, to be quite honest about it. All I wanted was to win one. The rest of them were bonuses. I never thought of medals, how many I had or how many I hadn't. One All-Ireland would have done me fine. At a young age I'd have died to put on the green and gold of Bennettsbridge and then the black and amber of Kilkenny. Winning medals never crossed my mind, it still doesn't. To have played for Kilkenny and to have played at a high standard, that made me quite happy.'

14. RAY CUMMINS

ON SUMMER SUNDAY EVENINGS IN THE LATE 1950S AND EARLY '60S THE BOYS OF
Ballinlough in Cork assembled for their weekly hurling contests. Those
warm summer evenings, young boys gathered on the Ballinlough Road
for the highlight of their week. It was there, on the street, that styles
were honed, skills learned, tricks shared and the first heat of battle
experienced by the young local hurlers.

As nightfall and the fading light brought those contests to a close,
yarns were spun, history evoked and the songs and legends of hurling
were recalled. It was there that the cream of future Blackrock teams
began their sporting journey. There too a young Ray Cummins, the
future Cork hurling captain and arguably the country's greatest dual
star, developed the talents that would win five senior All-Irelands in
both hurling and football, including a coveted hurling three-in-a-row.

'At that time Ballinlough was a suburb of Cork city,' Ray recalls. 'It
was quite close to the country. Once you went a mile down the road
you were out in the country. That time, of course, there weren't too
many cars around and we used to play hurling and football on the
street. We had matches there as intense as any I ever had in Croke
Park. That's where we learnt our hurling and football.

'On a Sunday evening it was traditional that we'd play up and down
what's known now as the Ballinlough Road. It's a very busy
thoroughfare now. But on Sunday evenings, after devotions, we had a
match up along the street. Then there was a little cottage owned by this
elderly man who was actually bedridden at the time, which we would
go to.

'Derry Cremin, who was the main motivator for under-age hurling
in Ballinlough and Blackrock at the time, used to go down to that

house on Sunday night. We'd all follow down, of course, after the match was over on the road. That's where we learnt our history and we listened to Seán Óg Ó Ceallacháin at eleven o'clock on a Sunday night for the results.

'The older guys would come back from the pub and there would be all kinds of arguments and discussions about who the best hurlers of various eras were, all that kind of thing. We were steeped in the tradition of hurling and the history of hurling from a very early age.'

In the late 1950s and early '60s the future of Cork hurling was secured in unofficial training grounds like the Ballinlough Road. Like many of his peers, Ray carried his hurling and football skills to the nearby Blackrock and St Michael's clubs. He also attended Coláiste Chríost Rí, where both he and his brothers Kevin, a future Cork minor, and Brendan, a future Cork senior, became part of the sporting success of the college.

It might seem likely that Ray Cummins' talent would have been noticed in the early 1960s at Cork under-age level but it didn't happen like that. At the time, Ray and his brother Brendan were winning all before them in under-age hurling and football. His other brother, Kevin, captained the Cork minors to an All-Ireland hurling championship in 1964. You would expect, therefore, that when Ray went for trial with the Cork U-15 hurlers, the outcome would be a foregone conclusion. But it wasn't to be. In one of the most notable hurling oversights, a future legend of the game was turned away.

'I remember going to the trial match for the Cork U-15 team,' Ray says. 'To tell you how good a team our club had, there were about seven or eight of us at the trial. I think, of the seven or eight that went, I was the only one that wasn't picked. Obviously, I was very disappointed over it. But I think, in later years, it stood me in good stead. At the time, I was determined that the next time I got a chance I was going to make it. By the time minor came around I got on the team. Maybe if I had got on the U-15 team I mightn't have been as determined later in life.'

A glance at the team-sheet for the 1966 All-Ireland minor hurling final, including the replay, shows just how well prepared for the future Cork were by the mid-1960s. Named against Wexford were players like John Horgan, Pat Moylan, Simon Murphy and Donal Clifford. Also on the team-sheet was Ray Cummins, who had recovered from his rejection at under-age level. Soon the Cork minors were becoming serial All-Ireland winners at minor hurling, while in the process producing future stars like Seán O'Leary and Jimmy Barry-Murphy.

Ray Cummins was by now playing hurling and football both at club level and for the Cork county minors. He soon graduated to the Cork U-21s in hurling and football, winning All-Ireland U-21 honours in hurling in 1968 and '69. He had by then moved to UCC, studying engineering, where he won Fitzgibbon Cup, Sigerson Cup and Cork county championship honours. Next came selection by the Cork seniors in both codes. Between club, college and county, at U-21 and senior levels, in both hurling and football, Ray Cummins' sporting life was little short of a blur.

'It was crazy at one stage particularly, when I was playing U-21,' Ray recalls. 'It was just a series of games, one after the other, week in week out. I found it tough going. There I was in college and that was difficult enough. But most of my spare time was taken up either training or playing matches.'

Somewhere along the way, at University College Cork, Ray Cummins switched to a position that he would make famous in the years to come. That position was full-forward. Initially playing as a half-back, his move to full-forward on the UCC hurling side came about virtually by accident, although he had prior experience of the role while playing club football. Tall, with a great sense of timing and vision, he chalked up scores with ease. He is remembered equally, however, for his capacity to roam, pluck the ball from the sky and feed other Cork forwards. Whatever option he chose, he did so with devastating effect.

'I was already playing with St Michael's as full-forward in football,' Ray says. 'When I went to college, naturally enough I played full-forward when I was playing with the footballers. At the time, Moss Keane was in college and he was playing full-back. When we were playing backs and forwards in training I had no chance against Moss. It was a case of me having to use brain rather than brawn. To avoid Moss, more than anything else, I started roaming.

'I was playing in the half-back line with the hurling team at the time and basically couldn't get on the team. I think they were short one night and they put me in full-forward. It took off from there. This was a time when the tradition was that you had the full-back and the full-forward raised up against each other inside the square. I had no chance that way. Physically I'm not as strong as a lot of the full-backs that were there at the time. I adopted this roaming play to get over that.'

Within months of his conversion to full-forward Ray Cummins was making his first appearance for the Cork seniors in the 1969 Munster hurling final. Cork won that day, defeating Tipperary. They also advanced to the All-Ireland final, where they lost to Kilkenny. Although tasting defeat, it was a day when Ray Cummins made history for a peculiar reason. 'I recall hearing Micheál O'Hehir making the point that it was the first time a helmet was worn in Croke Park,' Ray says. 'I had been playing with UCC and one of our players had got a serious head injury and had introduced the ice-hockey helmet for himself. Later on, I think, he started selling them.

'I never took to the visor. I found it very distracting and I found it very difficult to focus on the ball. Once it was on the ground it became very difficult with the bars of the visor. But I felt the one thing that was most important in hurling was to protect your head. I started to wear a helmet, as did Donal Clifford. The two of us were the first to wear them in Croke Park in the All-Ireland final of 1969.'

In 1970 Ray Cummins was back at Croke Park for his second All-Ireland hurling final appearance. This was once again a historic occasion, marking the first-ever 80-minute final. It was also historic in that Cork hammered 6–21 past a hapless Wexford who responded with their own remarkable, if flattering, tally of 5–10.

The relief in Cork was palpable. In the previous 15 years the Rebels had won just one senior hurling championship, back in 1966. The fans were starved for success. The pressure to succeed was immense. Cork fans, bedecked in red and white, helped swell the 65,000 who turned up in Croke Park on All-Ireland final day. This new Cork team, mixing the old in the form of captain and goalkeeper Paddy Barry, with the new in the shape of Ray Cummins, had caught the imagination of Cork supporters and brought relief to the Munster county.

'The homecoming for the winning Cork team was tremendous,' Ray recollects. 'That's probably what I remember most about it. It was my first time coming back with a winning team. Just to see the crowds in

Patrick Street as you turned into what was known then as Barry's corner, it was tremendous.

'In a county with a tradition like Cork's, there is a lot of expectation. There is a lot of pressure. But I played the game because I enjoyed it, because of the friends I made and because of the team spirit and the *craic* that you had with players. I never let it get too pressurised. OK, there was something wrong with you if you didn't go out on the field with butterflies in your belly. But, having said that, I tried to keep it in perspective.

'It wasn't the be-all and end-all of my life, as far as I was concerned. I had other things that were more important, like a job and, later on, a family. But I think you learn to handle pressure and when you have a good team around you, as I was fortunate to have, then you share the burden.

'When you get through a lot of hardship in training, rolling around in the mud in the middle of winter, which is the side of the game that a lot of the public don't see, it develops a tremendous bond among fellows and a tremendous determination to succeed. I think it lessens the pressure in the sense that you've got your work done and you just give it your all on the day.

'When you go out on the field, I think you have to focus so much that you don't actually hear the crowd. There are occasions during the match when you do but more often than not you're so focused on what you're doing that everything else is a blur around you. But Cork supporters are tremendous supporters. They're extremely loyal, extremely demanding as well. It's nice to know that you have the support of the county behind you. I think it gives you a bit of confidence as well, which is important.'

The Cork supporters and Ray Cummins were celebrating again in 1973 but this time in Gaelic football. That year Ray won his second senior All-Ireland medal in Cork's seven-point victory over Galway. They had previously beaten Kerry in the Munster final and would do so again in the Munster final of 1974.

By now Ray was recognised as a talented footballer, with performances that had already won him a football All-Star in 1971 to match the hurling All-Star he won the same year. He added a further football All-Star in 1973. That year he also became one of a select group of sportsmen to have won All-Ireland medals in both codes.

'The year 1973 was special to me even though I am a hurler by nature,' Ray says. 'I always consider myself as a hurler converted to football. I played football for enjoyment, for a break from the serious hurling side of it. But it was special in the sense that we had a tremendous bunch of players, some top-class players. We had unbelievable spirit among the team. It was also special in that it was 28 years since Cork had won an All-Ireland football final before that. I think it meant so much to the football pockets in Cork.

'I ended up taking frees. It wasn't my speciality. I wasn't expecting it on the day. As it turned out, it went OK. I probably had nightmares afterwards but when you're in the situation you don't think about these things, you just get on with it. I think it was such a confident team, anyway, that each individual felt that there was no mountain we couldn't climb. I don't think any of us could see ourselves being beaten that year. The aftermath was unbelievable and probably was our downfall the following year because we celebrated so much and we had so many nights out.'

They certainly value their hurling triumphs in Cork, no more so than the great three-in-a-row from 1976 to 1978. It was back in the 1950s, an era redolent with memories of Christy Ring, Paddy Barry and Willie John Daly, that the county previously achieved a similar feat. Now, in the latter half of the 1970s, Cork embarked on another great venture in one of the fondest chapters in the county's hurling history.

It was an era in Cork hurling that will long be remembered. That's partly because of the calibre of players featured on the various Cork teams: Jimmy Barry-Murphy, Seán O'Leary, Tom Cashman, Charlie McCarthy, Gerald McCarthy and Ray Cummins, to name but a few. It was also because of the team's style of play: the flair, the style and flamboyance that are a prerequisite to success in the view of Cork fans.

With victories over Wexford in 1976 and '77 and a further crucial defeat of Kilkenny in 1978, the Cork team of the late 1970s entered the realms of history. Ray Cummins played in all three campaigns, scoring memorable goals along the way. He also captained the team in their 1976 All-Ireland final victory over Wexford. That day, his brother Brendan played alongside him, his father Willie had manufactured the sliotars used in the final and his uncle, Bertie Walsh, drove the train carrying the victorious Rebels back to Cork.

'Wexford started off in a whirlwind and went something like two or three goals up in the first ten minutes,' Ray recalls of the first of the three-in-a-row finals. 'I said to myself: "My God, this is over now, anyway." But we slowly clawed our way back into the game and we had some tremendous displays. That was the day that Paddy Moylan scored something like ten points from play. Eventually, we overcame Wexford and I was as surprised as anyone that we got there at the end of the day.

'You win one All-Ireland and there's always a kind of desire to prove yourself. They say that you have to win two before you're accepted as a good team, particularly in Cork. There was a natural incentive in the second year to repeat it. Then, having done that, people talk about the three-in-a-row, which is another landmark in terms of All-Ireland wins. That drove us on for the next one.

'The team had tremendous spirit and a great bond. There is still a bond among the players. I mean, you had a rock-solid back line. Then you had some highly talented forwards that could score from all angles and would go through any kind of barrier to score a goal. I was very fortunate having Charlie McCarthy on one side and Seánie O'Leary on the other side. They were two fellows you could have just left the ball off to and you knew they were going to score.

'A lot of people would tell you that I didn't score any goals and I don't recall scoring a lot of them either. But I had the luxury of having Charlie and Seánie on both sides of me. It was probably easier for me to let it off to them and let them do the scoring rather than trying to score myself. I never really considered myself that skilful as a hurler but I used whatever attributes I had, my height or whatever, to get possession and basically let it off to the guys that had the skill.

'That team evolved over the three years and had different players and fresh players coming in. There was a very strong panel there and there were a lot of guys fighting for positions. I suppose that kept fellows on their toes as well. But we had a very good panel and I think that's what you need to win three All-Irelands. You need it now to win one All-Ireland but the depth of talent that we had in the panel was our strength, really.'

Ray Cummins had already retired from Gaelic football by the time he was winning his hurling medals in 1976, '77 and '78. 'Life was getting more serious,' he said. 'I had got married, was working at a job and I just felt I couldn't keep going. I couldn't give the commitment that was required. There was a danger of burn-out happening very quickly if I kept going with both of them. I was a hurler by nature and always preferred hurling and always will. I don't think I had much choice, really.'

For the rest of the 1970s and early '80s Ray continued with his inter-county hurling career. Those years were by no means unsuccessful, involving county, provincial and All-Ireland club victories with Blackrock. There were also further National Hurling League and Munster titles won with Cork. However, there would be no more All-Ireland victories up to his retirement following Cork's defeat by Kilkenny in the 1982 All-Ireland final.

'I remember running the length of Croke Park after Brian Cody and I was like an old dog chasing a young pup,' Ray says, regarding his decision to retire. 'It was unusual to run that distance as a full-forward and athleticism wasn't my strength. But I remember saying to myself that it's time to go. I had also felt a kind of pressure in that I wasn't enjoying it as much as I used to. I was finding it much harder and I was happy to go. I felt I had given them what I could for the years I was there. I had no regrets, really, and I haven't regretted it since.'

For almost half a century Ray Cummins and his family achieved some remarkable distinctions in the game of hurling. Ray's father, Willie, won All-Ireland minor titles in 1938 and '39, while playing with Christy Ring during the Cloyne hurler's early years. Ray's brother, Kevin, won an All-Ireland minor medal with Cork in 1964. His other brother, Brendan, shared in Ray's All-Ireland senior victory in 1976. With a mother who played camogie, the contribution of the Cummins family to Munster sport is hard to match.

On a personal level Ray won every honour and award in the game, including 11 successive Munster titles shared between hurling and football. There also were five All-Star awards, five senior All-Irelands and a host of medals won with UCC, Blackrock and with Munster in the Railway Cup. Yet it wasn't just the awards that singled Ray Cummins out but his unique dedication and commitment to Cork sport.

Ray Cummins shone as one of the finest dual stars in a county that produced great dual players like Teddy McCarthy, Jack Lynch and Jimmy Barry-Murphy. His achievements, allied to his sportsmanship and unselfish play, made him an acclaimed member of the hurling Team of the Millennium.

'I always had pride in the fact that I wore a Blackrock jersey and, equally, that I wore the Cork jersey,' Ray concludes. 'Both my club and my county had long and distinguished histories. You always felt an honour wearing the Cork jersey. It was not necessarily about winning trophies, even though it's nice to do so. To me, the game was all about teamwork. It's not just the players on the field but it's the mentors, the coaches, the groundsmen and the people that run the club and look after the youth. I think players should appreciate the honour they get when they represent the county. There are so many other players who'd love to do it and don't have the skills or don't have the opportunity to do so.

'They were marvellous days. I was lucky to be born in a hurling family, in a hurling parish and, obviously, in Cork with its hurling history. But to me, success was being involved. We had great fun and great friendships have developed over the years. It's lovely to know that you can go to Tipperary or Limerick or wherever and call in on your opponents, fellows that you played against, and you're welcome. You can have a bit of *craic*. The highlights for me were the *craic* that I had with the guys, whether it was training or playing, and the friends that I've made among both my team-mates and the guys I've played against. Those are the things that I cherish most about my career.'

15. JIMMY BARRY-MURPHY

ON THE MORNING OF 2 APRIL 1987 A FRONT-PAGE HEADLINE IN THE CORK EXAMINER announced the end of a superstar's career. The announcement, edged in black, was spread across page one in a style more familiar to the death of world leaders or the reporting of national tragedies. It made grim reading for legions of Cork hurling fans. After months of speculation, hurling's first superstar, the popular Jimmy Barry-Murphy, had retired from the game.

Fittingly, the morning paper mourned the loss of an astonishing sporting talent, winner of six All-Ireland senior medals, including five for hurling and one for football, along with seven All-Star awards and twelve Munster senior medals won in both codes. He was also, without doubt, the most charismatic all-rounder ever to wear the Rebel County colours.

That day in April 1987 Cork hurling lost more than just a fading hero. Since the early 1970s his face had appeared on Irish television screens, his rise to fame accompanying the arrival of colour TV and the age of super-heroes. Arms aloft, fists clenched and the ball in the net, no other hurler caught the mood or style of an era in quite the same way. Like the departure before him of George Best, in the years ahead fans would never again witness anything to match Jimmy Barry-Murphy.

Born in 1954, Jimmy was undoubtedly destined to achieve fame on the hurling and football stage. 'My family has a unique history in hurling in Cork, I suppose, in a lot of ways,' he remarks. 'My granduncle Dinny Barry-Murphy played with Cork in the 1920s. He captained Cork and won four All-Ireland medals. He played in that extraordinary 1931 final against Kilkenny, which went to three games.

My granduncle John also won an All-Ireland medal with Cork in the same period. I was reared on a diet of listening to stories about my granduncle Dinny and about my grandfather Finbarr, who also played with Cork and whom I knew very well through my father.

'My father went on to play with Cork in the 1940s and won a junior All-Ireland but didn't make the senior team. We have a long history with Cork, quite unique in many ways, and I grew up in an environment where sport was a huge part of our lives. It's from that I developed a great love of hurling and football, hurling in particular.

'I also played soccer and I loved that as well. I played with my local club, in my own area. But hurling was always my first love. I gravitated towards the 'Barrs under-age structure in Togher and it was a game that I was pretty useful at, at under-age level. I loved going to the games, going to Munster championship games when Cork were playing and going to the county finals in Cork, which were always huge. I loved playing soccer, as I said, but hurling was my main game.'

An All-Ireland winner in minor hurling in 1971, in minor football in '72 and in U-21 hurling in '73, it was, ironically, to senior soccer that Jimmy Barry-Murphy turned his attention in late 1972 and early '73. At the age of 18 he joined Cork Celtic, the losing FAI cup finalists in 1969 and a club very much living in the shadow of their local rivals, Cork Hibernians. However, Jimmy's tenure with Cork Celtic was brief, lasting a matter of weeks, after which he returned to his GAA roots at St Finbarr's.

'Towards the end of 1972, I was sent off in a club game in Cork against Glen Rovers and I received, I think, a two-month suspension. For that eight or ten weeks I was able to concentrate on my soccer activities. While playing with my local club, Wilton, I was approached by Cork Celtic. Paul O'Donovan, who was the manager at the time, asked me to give it a try. I said I would for a number of weeks. I knew that there was no great pressure on because the GAA season wasn't in full flight anyway and I must say I had a marvellous eight to ten weeks with Cork Celtic while it lasted. But it wasn't a particularly successful time for the team or for me, to be honest.'

Within months of his brief soccer career, both Jimmy, who was just 19, and his fellow Cork GAA footballers were marching to victory in a different football code at the All-Ireland final in Croke Park. They had already beaten Kerry in the Munster final by 5–12 to 1–15, the cornerstone of the victory being laid by two young stars, Barry-Murphy and Ray Cummins, both of whom would later excel as Cork hurlers. In the All-Ireland football final both players, led by Billy Morgan, again played their parts in Cork's seven-point victory over Galway. That was the day Barry-Murphy, who scored two goals, first tasted superstardom.

'I stopped playing soccer around the end of January 1973 and I was picked to play in a league game with Cork in the old Athletic Grounds. It was my first introduction, following on from my minor days, to the Cork senior scene. Really I knew very little about the scene, other than that Billy Morgan was the captain because Nemo had won the county championship. He was a player I had an awful lot of admiration for. I didn't know him particularly well. The coach, Donie O'Donovan, was a man of my father's vintage nearly at that time and he was quite an older man to be coaching the team, or so it appeared to me as a young lad coming on.

'We played a league game in the old Athletic Grounds in Cork and I was on and off the team then for a while. We didn't qualify for the knockout stages of the league. But prior to the first round of the championship, we were playing Clare in the Athletic Grounds again and while I didn't make the starting 15 I was included as a sub. Obviously, they had seen something in me and I was pushing pretty close to making the team. I was certainly in the panel, although I didn't come on in the game against Clare.

'I suppose it was a great surprise to many people when the team was announced for the Munster final and I was named at corner-forward. It created quite a lot of hype around Cork at the time because, I suppose, I played minor the previous year and it is unusual for minors to be playing so soon at senior level after that. My début in the Cork senior football team, in championship terms, was in the Munster final in the Athletic Grounds against Kerry, who had a very strong team and who were hot favourites going into the game.

'That was an extraordinary occasion, really, because we scored something like five goals in the first half. We just blitzed Kerry early on. It was remarkable in the sense that myself and Ray Cummins alternated positions. I was picked in the corner and Ray was picked full-forward but we alternated. I played full-forward and Ray played in the corner and we seemed to upset the Kerry backs in some fashion by doing that. It was fantastic. It was one of those days when nothing went wrong for us and the second half was just a matter of playing out time.

'It was all new to me and I was amazed at the hype and the expectations that it created. Cork hadn't won an All-Ireland since 1945, so here we were looking forward to the chance of winning an All-Ireland for the first time since '45. I suppose a lot of the media attention, some of it certainly, came onto myself because I was the youngest player on the team. A lot of the players had been around the Cork scene for a long time and hadn't won an All-Ireland medal. A lot of interest was generated in me because of that.

'To get to the All-Ireland final in 1973 against Galway created huge hype in Cork. Walking out at Croke Park was fantastic. I can't describe it. It was the old Croke Park then; it's much changed nowadays. The dressing-rooms were under the old Cusack Stand at that time. It was a very wooden structure and you could hear the sounds reverberating through from the minor game. I'd played in the minor final the previous year, of course, and I wasn't sure what the senior final held for me.

'To be perfectly honest with you, looking back on it, I had very little nerves. I can't remember having a trace of nerves at all on the big day. I was very confident. I suppose the brashness of youth gives you that confidence. There's no fear. You haven't been there before, so you don't know what the pitfalls are.

'Undoubtedly, it is a special occasion for me to look back on, a landmark in my career which put me on the national stage in a big way. I scored two goals and a point and, I suppose, that team has always been revered in Cork as a very special team, obviously because of the gap from the previous victory to that one. But the irony of the whole thing is that, having won the final, I thought this is going to be easy, we'll be here in the finals for the next ten years. I was never to play in a football final again. It just goes to show that the exuberance of youth and the confidence of youth can carry you a long way.'

In the mid-1970s few observers could have predicted the forthcoming revival in Cork's hurling fortunes that was about to take place. Already a double All-Star for football, Jimmy Barry-Murphy was now playing hurling with style for his club, St Finbarr's, and for the Cork senior hurling team. He showed remarkable form in his new role, pumping in goals and points for the 'Barrs in the county and All-Ireland club hurling championships while winning praise for his appearances in the Cork senior hurling side.

In the 1975 hurling championship Cork reached the All-Ireland semi-final, where, despite a goal from Jimmy, they lost to Galway. The following year Cork's path to Croke Park was secured through victories over Tipperary and Limerick. Facing Wexford in the 1976 All-Ireland final, the Rebels arrived in Dublin as underdogs, tipped to fail by press and radio alike. Few spotted the turning point in Cork's hurling fortunes which that 1976 final was about to bring.

Starting on the wing that day, Jimmy Barry-Murphy had an inauspicious game up to the last quarter. Despite goals by Ray Cummins and Charlie McCarthy, the outcome was in doubt up to late in the second half. However, an inspired switch of Barry-Murphy from the wing to the half-forward line, where he faced the impressive Wexford centre-back Mick Jacob, transformed the game. The final score in 1976: Cork 2–21, Wexford 4–11.

The result that day not only won for Barry-Murphy an All-Ireland hurling medal to match the football medal won three years earlier but it also set in train an extraordinary run of three successive All-Ireland hurling triumphs. The following year brought hurling medal number two, this time in a second successive victory over Wexford. Then in 1978 came the third medal in a row with defeat of the old enemy, Kilkenny, by 1–15 to 2–8, the Cork goal being scored by the team's now-established superstar, Barry-Murphy.

'When I came on the Cork team I was playing wing-forward. That was because the team was very strong and you had a full-forward line of Charlie McCarthy, Ray Cummins and Seánie O'Leary. That was a fantastic full-forward line and obviously I wasn't in a position to get into it. The Cork selectors were deploying some of us in other places. It was only in my latter years, after Ray Cummins retired, that full-forward became my position.

'When I was playing wing-forward I wasn't happy out there. Closer to goal was always my game and both in my club and county I was much happier playing full-forward than anywhere else. I loved playing full-forward because you're in the thick of the action. Goal chances come there. I just loved playing close to goal and I always said it was my favourite position.

'In the 1976 final I had a very peripheral part for a lot of the game because I was playing wing-forward and I wasn't having a particularly good game. Mick Jacob, who was playing centre-back for Wexford on that occasion, was having an outstanding game and I was moved in on him with about 15 minutes to go. I proceeded to score four or five points. It seemed to be a turning point in the game and again luck seemed to go my way. I think, in fairness, he was probably tiring at that stage and I got a couple of breaks, scored a few points and we won the All-Ireland.

'Of the three games, Cork and Kilkenny was the crunch game. It always is because the bottom line is that Kilkenny have a very good record against Cork over the years. Historians will tell you that their record against us is well in favour of Kilkenny and quite a number of those victories were by the slimmest of margins, a point. It's something that Kilkenny people don't ever let us forget or live down. I think the rivalry is fantastic and it's very healthy. When you're playing on a Cork team it's very special to beat Kilkenny. That certainly was the key one because I don't think outside of Cork the team would have been regarded as highly if we hadn't beaten Kilkenny as part of that three-in-a-row.

'When you look back on it, the three-in-a-row team of '76, '77 and '78 was a remarkable achievement. It hasn't been done since. It's a very, very difficult thing to do with most of the same body of players. But I would say the strength of the team was its many diverse parts. We had an outstanding team of 18 or 20 individuals. We all played different parts on different days.

'We had players who would be outstanding in any era, like Gerald McCarthy, Ray Cummins, John Horgan, Denis Coughlan, Charlie McCarthy. They were players who would adorn any Cork team. Some players were probably coming towards the end of their careers but an infusion of new blood like myself, Tom Cashman, Dermot McCurtain, Johnny Crowley and Seánie O'Leary had a huge impact. It was the sum of all the parts together. The team just welded together beautifully and it was a unique time for Cork hurling.'

The prospects of Cork achieving four in a row foundered in 1979 when they surprisingly lost to Galway in the All-Ireland semi-final. Although that defeat was somewhat tempered by Cork's fifth successive Munster final victory, the following year they relinquished their run of victories in Munster, losing to Limerick in a thrilling Munster final. The next year again, 1981, Cork won the National Hurling League. However, in the Munster semi-final Cork hurling fans watched their team lose to Clare for the first time in over a quarter of a century of championship hurling.

Clearly the burden of expectation rested heavily on Cork hurlers when, in 1982 and '83, they returned once more to Croke Park to contest two highly charged All-Ireland finals. With Jimmy Barry-Murphy installed as captain, predictions in 1982 were that Cork would ease past their age-old rivals, Kilkenny. But it was not to be. In fact, a rampant Kilkenny won both All-Irelands, in 1982 and '83, adding insult to injury by becoming National Hurling League champions in both years as well.

'I was captain of Cork,' Jimmy recalls. 'We had won the county championship and so I had the honour of captaining the Cork team, which is the way it works in Cork. In other counties the team manager picks the captain. But in Cork the captain comes from the county champions. I was lucky enough to be given the honour in both those years.

'I suppose it had always been a major ambition of mine to captain Cork and to win an All-Ireland. I probably made a mistake of saying that publicly along the way, which generated its own publicity and hype. I certainly should have kept that quiet. But it was a significant ambition and it was something I craved and longed to do.

'The defeats were particularly disappointing and hard to take because I didn't play particularly well on either occasion. I have to hold my hands up and admit I didn't deliver on the day and we were beaten by Kilkenny on both occasions. It was very hard to take at the time but you learn to live with it. You look back on your career and you say you had many great occasions. But you've got to learn to live with the bad ones and get over them. You've got to be man enough to hold your hands up and say you didn't have a good day and just get on with it.'

In the following three seasons Jimmy Barry-Murphy added two

further All-Ireland hurling medals to his rapidly growing collection. His fourth hurling medal came in 1984, the GAA's centenary year, when Cork travelled to Thurles and beat Offaly by 3–16 to 1–12. Having lost to Galway in the 1985 semi-final, Cork turned the tables the following year when Jimmy won his fifth All-Ireland hurling final, beating Galway 4–13 to 2–15. That successful championship season turned out to be Jimmy Barry-Murphy's last in the red and white of Cork.

'Cork teams, I think, seem to have a knack of winning finals in special years. I suppose every county wanted to win the centenary final. A huge factor, of course, was playing Tipperary in the Munster final in Thurles. It was a great achievement to go and beat them there. Then, the very fact of the All-Ireland final being staged in Thurles, which traditionally has been a happy hunting-ground for Cork, was a huge incentive for the team. I think we had a very good day and, in fairness to Offaly, they had a bad day. It was quite a facile win in the end, really.

'That team, more or less, went on to win another final in 1986. I think it's fair to say we bounced back from the defeats in '82 and '83 and showed a lot of character to do that. I think that the '84 final, in particular, was a great win. In '86, with practically the same team and a couple of new players coming in, it was a great achievement again to go on and beat Galway.'

Having retired in 1987, Jimmy Barry-Murphy initially became a part-time television analyst but eventually returned to the Cork hurling scene. At first he coached the minors at St Finbarr's, followed by the county minors whom he led to All-Ireland success in 1995, culminating in his appointment as coach of the Cork senior hurling team. National Hurling League winners in 1998, the young Cork players, for whom Jimmy's exploits in the Cork jersey were regarded with awe, soon emerged on the national stage. It all came to a head in 1999 when the Cork senior side achieved All-Ireland success, defeating Kilkenny on a dark, rainy day at Croke Park by 0–13 to 0–12. By the narrowest of margins the fortunes of his years as captain in 1982 and '83 had been reversed.

'I had, I suppose, been too public in my utterance about wanting to captain the Cork team in the 1980s. So when I started coaching I was too afraid to think that I'd be lucky enough to coach a team to win an All-Ireland. The victory in 1999 certainly made up for that. The players gave me a tremendous day. It was the greatest day of my life.

'It was great for me to be there as part of a young Cork team, going to Croke Park with colleagues like Tom Cashman, who had been a great support to me in my playing days and then subsequently in my coaching days. It was great to be there with a management team of ex-Cork players, with the supporters and what it meant to the people of Cork. The public really took to us. I'll never be able to thank this particular group of players for the honour they gave me in Croke Park that day. It was really unique and I'll never forget it.'

Shortly after Cork's surprise loss to Offaly in the semi-final of the 2000 championship Jimmy Barry-Murphy retired from the Cork hurling scene. He walked away with five All-Ireland senior hurling medals and one for senior football. In both hurling and football he also won a grand total of seven All-Star awards, three National League medals, 12 Munster medals and a rake of national and county medals won with his club, St Finbarr's.

Among his many career highlights were the stunning four goals he scored for Munster footballers against Ulster in the 1975 Railway Cup final. There also was his famous goal scored while doubling on a John Fenton ball during the All-Ireland semi-final against Galway in 1983, a shot many regard as one of the finest ever witnessed in Croke Park. In addition, in 1980 he became the first player in history to win National League hurling and football medals. Perhaps more importantly, however, he departed with his reputation intact as one of the most unassuming all-rounders in the history of Irish sport.

'I think "superstar" is a misnomer in lots of ways. Superstars, to me, are huge TV stars, film stars, rock stars, mega-soccer players in Britain and on the Continent, who earn massive amounts of money. I think we're involved in a smaller scene in the GAA here in Cork and in Ireland. The media interest over the past number of years has increased greatly, obviously. But I never considered myself a "superstar" in any sense of the word whatsoever. I'm fairly well known in Cork, I suppose, but I think terms like "superstar" would be an exaggeration. I was lucky enough to play on an excellent team and I never saw myself as anything other than that.

'You are lucky to be born in a county like Cork. It's a big county with a great hurling tradition. There's a great sense of pride in being picked to play for Cork at any level. But in particular, a senior hurler and a senior All-Ireland medal-holder in Cork is accorded a certain respect and status, particularly if the public take to you and you show a certain humility. What we do in Cork then is try and build on that tradition and use it to our advantage to win further All-Irelands.

'As for the medals, I'm not a person who likes to have these things hanging around the walls, adorning my walls at home. Everyone does their own thing with these things. Medals are great to have but I don't look back and say how many medals do I have or how many the guy I'm talking to has, four, five or six All-Ireland medals. They don't mean a lot. I don't think it really matters how many you have. Many great players didn't win All-Ireland medals at all; that's the point I'm trying to make. It's how you're remembered, how you played the game, what kind of contribution you made to the game, the friendships you made over the years, that's what matters.'

16. JOE COONEY

ONE OF THE MOST CURIOUS BATTLES IN CLUB HURLING HISTORY TOOK PLACE IN THE TOWN of Ballinasloe, County Galway, in February 1990. It was played on a bleak day, with a dark sky and blustery wind, with heavy rain causing flooded roads. The contestants were Sarsfields, from nearby New Inn and Bullaun, who travelled just down the road for the match. Their opponents were Ballyhale Shamrocks, who came from much further afield in County Kilkenny.

Neutral spectators at that All-Ireland club semi-final might have been forgiven if they glanced twice at the team-sheets. In fact, they might have been excused if they thought the match was some kind of inter-family contest. For that day seven Fennellys, stretching from goal right up to the forwards, dominated the Kilkenny team. Facing them were six of the Cooneys from Galway, including 1987 Hurler of the Year, Joe Cooney.

'I have good cause to remember that one,' Joe says. 'It was early February and it was very, very wet. We got a couple of very wet weeks before that match, which was played in Ballinasloe. It's not our local club but it's down the road. The match was fixed for two o'clock or so and I remember going early that day to collect my wife, who was my girlfriend then.

'On the way I got caught in a flood and the car broke down. I couldn't get going. This fellow in Athenry had a filling-station and, lucky enough, he was going to the match as well. He had to wait until somebody came to take over from him. He gave me a lift down and I ended up being about five minutes late.

'The team had been picked, they were out on the field and the game was on when I arrived. The fellows had been playing so well that they didn't know who to take off. I had to sit there and watch it. I was eventually brought on after ten minutes or so. I think we were beaten by two points but I suppose it was a game we could have won if things had gone differently.

'There were seven Fennellys playing and they were very good. For us, my brother Jimmy was playing and Brendan and Pakie were the full-back line. Michael was centre-back. Peter was corner-forward and I was supposed to be playing centre-forward. Between us, there was half of the team on both sides. It was a great day for both families because it isn't often that happens.

'It's great to see it happening. There's a lot of players that mightn't get a chance to play at county level and they get a chance to show what they're capable of at club level. At the end of the day, the club is what it's all about. That's where it starts and that's where it's going to finish. That's why we were always delighted to be able to play for our club. We were going to give it 100 per cent every day we went out.'

Few families contributed more to their club or county than the Cooneys of Galway. With an uncle, Paddy Fahy, who played both hurling and football for Galway, and a father who hurled with the local Sarsfields, it was inevitable that the family would be immersed in sport. For the six boys in a family of fourteen, hurling soon became their sport of choice.

Whether in the yard at home, in the nearby fields or in the local Sarsfields club, the young Cooneys applied themselves to the job of perfecting their hurling skills. In time, four of the brothers developed as backs, the others developed as forwards. Two, Jimmy and Joe, played for Galway; two more were on the senior county panel. All six played for Sarsfields, a tiny club that went on to unprecedented All-Ireland success. With a hinterland of no more than 250 houses, Sarsfields eventually won All-Ireland club championships in 1993 and '94. It says something of the Cooney family that the brothers provided the backbone of the team that won both of those finals.

'There was a big family of us in it,' Joe remarks. 'At the back of our house there was a kind of shed with a hole in the wall. It was maybe two foot by two foot and we used to be practising taking frees, seeing who could get the ball through the hole. If you could do that, you were doing well. Then there were other smaller air holes down along the line and, if you were very good, you could get them in the small ones. But that wasn't easy to do.

'We used to play one fellow in goals and maybe two lads out the field. One would be marking the other, trying to take the ball off one another. We spent a lot of time at that in the garden and I suppose it helped us a lot. Then there was a gable-end at the side of the house and we used to practise there all the time, hitting the ball up against the wall and catching it and trying to do different stuff with it. It all stood to us when the years went on.

'You never were stuck for anyone to play with. There was always someone around. Anytime we got a chance we always had the ball and the hurl in our hands and we were pucking it over and back to one another. We often had games between ourselves as well. Then we had the neighbours. There were a few up the road and beside us. We nearly had a 15-a-side game at times. It was very easy to get people to play with you at that time. Times have changed an awful lot since then.'

The big time began for the Cooneys back in 1980 when big brother Jimmy won a rare All-Ireland medal. The event was rare because it marked the first Galway success in the championship in 57 years. It also was unusual and memorable for the outpouring of emotion that greeted the players in Croke Park and back in Eyre Square. From that team came some great exponents of hurling, especially John Connolly. Having a brother Jimmy on the same side as John Connolly and other Galway stars was any young boy's dream.

'Jimmy is about ten years older than me,' Joe says. 'I saw him playing league games and saw him playing club championship matches. He was always very good. What I used to say is, hopefully, some day I might be able to do the same thing. I thought that I'd never get as far as he got but you never feel a few years slipping by. He really got the ball rolling, I suppose, in one sense.

'When you'd be watching matches, you'd pick out someone and you'd just watch what he'd do for the game and see if maybe you could do that as well. John Connolly was one of the fellows that I used to just sit and watch. I was amazed by what he could do. There were other fellows as well. There were the likes of Sylvie Linnane. There was P.J. Molloy. There were some very, very good hurlers. You'd go home and you'd try those things out and see could you do them. We all have our own heroes but those were the players that I really enjoyed watching and tried to emulate as I moved on.'

Three years after Jimmy picked up his All-Ireland medal young Joe Cooney was playing for the Galway minors in his own All-Ireland final. At the time few realised how that minor team of 1983 would set the scene for Galway's great run of senior success later on in the decade. In 1983, however, the no-little matter of Dublin had to be overcome in the minor final. At the core of that Dublin side was a young hurler by the name of Niall Quinn.

'While it wasn't one of the best finals, we came out on top,' Joe recalls. 'There was a fellow playing with Dublin I heard about called Niall Quinn. He had scored something like three goals and four points in a Leinster final against Wexford, which is a very hard thing to do. I knew that if we were going to win an All-Ireland we'd have to watch out for this fellow and someone had to mark him very closely.

'We happened to be on top a good bit out the field and he didn't get as much ball as normal. But all I remember is that a puck-out came. I don't think the ball even hit the ground but Niall Quinn pulled at it in the middle of the field and put it straight over the bar. It was one of the best scores that I have ever seen. He was a fellow that had huge potential as a hurler but we all know what he has gone on to since. If he had stuck with it he'd have definitely made it big.'

The Galway breakthrough in senior hurling took off in earnest in 1985 when the county reached the first of four-in-a-row All-Ireland finals. By then the best of the successful county minors from 1983 had begun to appear on the senior panel. Diligent preparation and training also were having an impact. Encouraged by the victory in 1980, fortified by the influx of new young players and blessed with a strong mix of talent, the Tribesmen embarked on a venture that had never been experienced before in Galway hurling.

'In 1980 Cyril Farrell took over the Galway team and he really did a lot of work with them,' Joe says. 'Times were changing as regards training systems and the amount of time that was spent on training. I think he brought a kind of professionalism into it and it really got going from there. They won the All-Ireland in 1980 and they were unlucky in 1981 that they didn't win another one. I suppose from there it started.

'We had a minor team in '83 which, again, Cyril Farrell was involved in. Off that team maybe seven or eight fellows made it on to the senior panel a few years after. It is not too often that happens, you know. You might be lucky to get two or three off any team. Plus you had the likes of Pete Finnerty, Tony Keady, Sylvie Linnane, Conor Hayes, the Kilkennys; very good players like that. They were around at that time. There was a great nucleus there of good players, plus the young fellows that came from the minor team.

'In '85, then, it really started. We went up to Croke Park to play Cork in a semi-final. It was a really wet day. You could see the water on Croke Park that day; it was splashing every time anyone would run. We won that match and it was a big upset because Cork had a very settled team. They were very good at the time. We happened to get on top of them and we got a couple of goals that really put us in the driving seat. We went on, then, and we were beaten by Offaly in the final. It could have gone any way at the time. I suppose that was the start of it.'

Two disappointing All-Ireland defeats later and Galway followers could be forgiven for wishing that the team had stayed west of the Shannon. Having lost by two points to Offaly in the 1985 final, Galway then lost to Cork in the following year's decider by a margin of four points. Side by side with the seniors, however, the Galway U-21 side were making progress and in 1986, with Joe Cooney starting as full-forward, they defeated Wexford in the U-21 All-Ireland final. Although a senior for two years at that stage, and despite the team's stylish and prolific forwards, Joe Cooney and the Galway senior revival had yet to fully bear fruit.

'I suppose it was a learning process, really, when you look back at it,' Joe says, recalling the defeats of 1985 and '86. 'You would be very disappointed after being beaten in two All-Ireland finals one year after the next. But we really learned from that. We knew at the time that we had a good outfit and that if things changed a bit for us that we could go ahead and win one or two. And that's what happened: the next two years after that we won All-Irelands.'

Galway's roller-coaster ride in 1987 was a remarkable one by any hurling standards. That year they won the National Hurling League and the All-Ireland final, defeating Kilkenny in the championship decider. Joe Cooney won an All-Star award and was honoured as Hurler of the Year. His province also won the Railway Cup with an all-Galway line-up, defeating Leinster, in Ennis, by 2–14 to 1–14.

The year 1988 brought another senior All-Ireland for Joe Cooney and Galway, following victory over Tipperary. That year the Tribesmen also appeared in the first of six Oireachtas finals in a row. They won five, suffering defeat only to Tipperary in 1990. How the tide had turned for Galway hurling! Just as importantly, how the prospect of a third All-Ireland defeat in a row had been avoided in that anxious, low-scoring final against Kilkenny in 1987!

'When you were beaten twice, in two All-Ireland finals, there's one thing that you're not going to let happen and that is you're not going to be beaten in a third one,' Joe emphasises. 'I think we really knuckled down at the start of the year and we got together and said that this wasn't going to happen again. We had learned a lot. We were young in the previous two years. I suppose we thought things were going to happen for us and they just didn't. You had to go out and make them happen and I think that's what we did in 1987.

'I was lucky that year to get Hurler of the Year because of where we were and the team were so good at the time. You'll get years like that. No matter how good a hurler you are, if you're not seen in the semi-finals or finals of All-Irelands you're not going to get the awards. I think that's where your team comes into play. If your team is going well, you get more television coverage and everyone sees you. They could have given it to any one of 12 players that year but I happened to get it. It's a lovely award to get. It's a great recognition. But I think, at the end of the day, once your team wins the All-Ireland and once you get your All-Ireland medal, that's what it's all about.

'We had been around for a good while. We had learned a lot. When you get a team playing together for a good number of years you get into a pattern and everyone knows what everyone is doing and what should be done. I think things come easier to you and you don't panic as much as you might. You'll try to be doing too much when you're younger and things won't work out for you. Your experience helps a lot after that. I think that's what happened to us in 1987 and '88. You have to go through the losing side of it before you'll really appreciate the wins that you get after that.'

There were two more years left in the great Galway team of the 1980s but unfortunately there were no further championship triumphs. The 1989 campaign was notable for Galway's exit in an ill-tempered semi-final clash with Tipperary. It also was remembered for the notorious Tony Keady affair involving the suspension of the Galway hurler for playing in the USA. 'It was unfortunate for him,' Joe says, 'because it put a damper on a great career. There have been a lot of players that played out there and got away with it. He was just one of the high-profile players that got caught.'

There was one last hurrah for the team in 1990. Having disposed of Offaly in the semi-final, the Tribesmen advanced to the All-Ireland final against Cork. That was the day when Ger Cunningham's massive puck-outs put pressure on Galway. It was also the day when Joe Cooney, who was captain, put in an outstanding performance. Unfortunately for Joe and for Galway, the scoreline favoured Cork by a remarkable 5–15 to 2–21.

'It was a great honour to lead your team out in 1990 and I was hoping things would work out,' Joe says. 'Any time I'm captain of a team, it doesn't seem to be lucky. That day, going in at half-time, we were well up, well on top and we were hurling well. Everywhere I went the ball seemed to come after me and things were going great.

'Ten minutes into the second half we were well ahead and Martin Naughton soloed in with the ball and he took a shot and hit Ger Cunningham on the nose. It went out for a sixty-five but we didn't get the sixty-five. The puck-out came and they got a goal below. Small things like that can change the whole course of the game and we ended up 2–21 to 5–15.

'It was a massive score. Every few minutes there was a score coming. It was probably one of the most enjoyable finals. If you were a Cork person, it was one of the most enjoyable finals anyhow. But in our case it was very disappointing after playing so well and still being beaten. But that's it, there's nothing you can do about it now. It was a big disappointment being captain as well. It's a devil of a thing to happen like that, you know.

'When you're young and you're there four or five times, you'll say it's only a matter of time before you'll win another one. We even said that in 1990. But a lot of time passed and Galway won nothing.

You've got to take your chances when they come and we didn't do that.'

Throughout his career Joe Cooney was known for his speed, his great sense of position, his scoring ability and those darting runs that tore opposing defences to pieces. Although he shone on the big stage, in many ways it was the two successive All-Ireland club championships in the 1990s that helped define his career. Exposure with Galway may have brought his unique talent to national attention but it was the club that marked out Joe's family roots in the community in Bullaun. That the tiny area served by Sarsfields achieved two successive All-Ireland titles was, in itself, an extraordinary record. That so many Cooneys contributed to the successes was also unique.

On the national stage Joe Cooney returned for a further shot at All-Ireland glory in 1993 but his side was unlucky to lose to Kilkenny. He ended up, however, with two senior All-Irelands, three National Hurling Leagues and four Railway Cup medals. His Hurler of the Year award was also accompanied by five All-Star awards, which were won at the height of his hurling career. He played on for many years after but it was really those golden years in the latter half of the 1980s and the top of the 1990s that he's remembered for, as a star of the great Galway sides that made six All-Ireland appearances.

'Sometimes, when you turn on the TV or listen to the radio, you'll hear people talking and they'll pick out maybe 10 or 15 good players. It's always nice when your name is mentioned and it gives a lot of satisfaction. I'm not a great one for sitting down watching videos of games or looking at matches that I'd have played. But if a match comes on television and I happen to be watching it's always nice to say: "God, I was there and I played in that one." Little bits and pieces would come back to you after seeing it again.

'It's a big change going to a game now, say at county level, and looking out at fellows on the field. You'd be kind of saying: "I'd do this or that now if I was there." You'd see them doing something different and you'd say: "Why didn't he do it that way?" But all players are different and everyone is unique in their own way. It's a thing that you've just got to get used to. I'm delighted going watching matches now. I've really settled into the retirement scene.

'I think all good teams come to an end, the great Kerry football team as well. You'll get your time at the top and you've got to take it. If you don't, you'll be sorry forever. We won two and we possibly could have won more with the team we had. But there again, how many other good teams have never won anything? We're delighted with the two that we did win.'

17. JOE DOOLEY

IT WOULD BE HARD TO FIND A FAMILY MORE COMMITTED TO THE SPORT OF HURLING THAN the Dooleys of Offaly. For almost two decades, three of the family, Joe, Billy and Johnny, played for their county at various times and at the highest level. Their career achievements, either separately or together, include Offaly's All-Ireland successes of 1985, '94 and '98. A fourth brother, Kieran, occasionally togged out in his county's colours. Along with a fifth brother, Séamus, the family also represented their club, Seir Kieran, with distinction in various county championships.

Like the Rackards with Wexford in the 1950s, the Dooleys helped form the backbone of Offaly's astonishing success in the 1980s and '90s. Together with other Offaly families like the Whelahans, the Troys and the Pilkingtons, they imprinted their name on the Faithful County's golden era. Almost impossible to imagine was the sheer intensity of the family's commitment. Along with the relentless training was the expense, the preparation of gear, the travelling to matches, the media attention, the forfeiting of holidays and the almost complete sublimation of family life to the cause of the club and the county.

'I suppose hurling is number one, really, in all our lives,' Joe, the eldest of the Dooleys, says. 'My father and mother both had hurling in their families. My father's uncle, Tom Dooley, played in a junior All-Ireland in 1929. On my mother's side, her father and her uncle played with Offaly in a junior All-Ireland in 1923. Hurling was all that was talked about. Right from the time we were able to walk, we were talking about hurling. Our main objective would be to grow up and play hurling for the club and for Offaly.

'Everywhere I went as a young fellow I always had a hurl in my hand. Going out to bring in the cows, or going to school or coming back from school, no matter where I went, going to the bog, I always carried a hurl with me. Anyone who knows me would confirm that. My father always brought me to games as a young fellow. When you'd come home in the evenings, you'd be out hurling stones over the wall and pretending to be whoever you saw that day on the field.

'I had four brothers, Séamus, Kieran, Billy and Johnny, and we all played hurling. There were always great games at home in the yard, in the evening times or at weekends. We had a field out the back and we put up our own goals and nets and we'd make up our own games. We'd have a few of the neighbours in as well. There was often skin and hair flying. Many's the game that didn't finish, that ended up in a row or one thing or another. But we all stuck at it, anyway. Any rows we had, we kept them among ourselves.

'Séamus was a hard style of hurler but he was interested. Kieran was very talented but probably didn't have the go in him that both Billy and Johnny had. Kieran played a few league games with Offaly. But to play with the county you have to have a huge determination and a will to succeed. Both Billy and Johnny showed that from an early age and you could see that both of them were going to make it. You can do so much on the training field but if anyone really wants to make it they have to put in the effort every spare minute they get.

'I suppose hurling became number one in all our lives. We all now have family lives and work but outside of that hurling is the most important thing. Holidays and everything else are put to one side. When the hurling season is over, then you can think about taking a holiday but not before then. To illustrate that, a couple of years ago my wife organised a holiday for the first two weeks in November because we said there won't be anything on at that time of the year. But, to make a long story short, we got to the All-Ireland final in 1998 and the club championship resumed after the All-Ireland. We weren't going that well early in the year but suddenly, in September, we started to pick up a bit and we were winning games. I could see a collision course coming up with the holiday and the county final.

'It was the first time we ever had a family holiday together. The kids were nine or ten at the time. We flew out to the Canaries on the Monday and the county final was for the following Sunday. There was no way it was being postponed. I had to fly home on the Friday for the county final and come back on the Monday. We played the county final on the Sunday and I rang Marie after the match and I said: "I've got good news and bad. The good news is that we didn't lose. The bad news is we didn't win. It was a draw and the replay is next Sunday." Needless to say, she wasn't too impressed. But things worked out. That's the kind of thing. I was expected to come home that year. There was no question of me not coming home and the club and everybody would have expected it.

'You can't give anything less than 100 per cent if you're involved, if you want to succeed. The lads would say the same thing as well. They would have made the same commitment. There would be no such thing as planning a holiday for June or July or any time during the summer. Both Billy and Johnny got married, I think, in May and late September, respectively. There was no point in planning it at any other time of the year because it would get in the way of training.

'I think any of the players involved with Offaly that got married would have married in the off-season. If affects your whole family life, really. But I don't think any of them would complain about it. We've had a lot of success and a lot of great trips and a lot of great memories, and they're the things you have to look back on. Making friends and getting to know people all over the country, I suppose that's what it's all about.'

The initial rise of Offaly in the early 1980s came a little too soon for the Dooley family's burgeoning hurling skills. At the turn of the new decade Joe, the eldest, was 16. Séamus and Kieran, the next two in line, were 15 and 13, respectively. Billy, who came next, was 11. Johnny, who was the last in line of the boys, was only just nine. Despite being too young to participate, however, they certainly were old enough to savour the drama of Offaly's emergence from the hurling wilderness.

Literally from nowhere, with no previous senior success to their credit, Offaly stormed to a Leinster championship victory in 1980 by defeating Kilkenny. The following year they did it again, defeating Wexford. Warming to the theme, in 1981 they travelled to Croke Park for the All-Ireland final, where they beat Galway. Understandably, the county was alight with excitement. For a family with boys whose ages were bunched in the teens and pre-teens, the enthusiasm for hurling was infectious.

'In the spring of 1980 I would have been 16 and I can recall being outside mass one Sunday morning in Clareen,' Joe says. 'Usually, everyone would hang around and we'd have a bit of a chat for maybe 10 or 15 minutes. Somebody commented that maybe Offaly was going to win the Leinster championship that year. It was kind of greeted with a laugh. Little did we think that Offaly would go on and win the Leinster championship.

'I can remember it very well. I was at the game and there were only 8,500 people there. We went up on the bus from Clareen. I can still remember Mark Corrigan and Paddy Kirwan scoring the points and Johnny Flaherty's goals. Everybody played out of their skins that day. The game was talked about, I'd say non-stop, for two weeks afterwards. Then Offaly went on and won the All-Ireland in 1981.

'They had no All-Ireland semi-final in 1981. They went straight into the All-Ireland final. I remember being at the match and being behind the goals in the Canal End and seeing Johnny Flaherty scoring the winning goal. I was right behind it with my father. It was hugely exciting times for Offaly. We had made the breakthrough and I don't think anybody in their wildest dreams would have believed that Offaly was going to win an All-Ireland even six or seven months before that. It was unreal stuff, really.

'I started with Offaly six months later, in March of 1982. I was lucky to come in on the back of that. Like, it would be the equivalent now of Westmeath or Laois coming through and winning an All-Ireland. It was very exciting times for Offaly and for me as well. The rest of the family were a good bit younger. Johnny and Billy were coming behind and they were watching all this. But we were close to the scene during those early years in the '80s and probably through myself they would have seen first-hand what it was like.'

In 1984, at the age of 20, Joe Dooley made his championship début against Wexford. By now Offaly was an epicentre of hurling activity. Back in 1981 their star player, Pat Delaney, was awarded the honour of Hurler of the Year. The county seniors, with Joe Dooley on board, were preparing for two further All-Ireland appearances that would bring defeat by Cork in 1984 and victory over Galway in 1985. To crown it all, the county minors were about to storm to two minor successes in 1986 and '87. In all those matches the name Dooley would appear prominently. It was the beginning of the Dooley family dominance in Offaly hurling.

'The first All-Ireland that I played in was in '84, in Thurles against Cork,' Joe recalls. 'Johnny went to the game with my father and he tells me himself that my father got him in over the stiles. He wasn't a small young lad at the time but he managed to get him in. Those were the days when officialdom wasn't as strict as it is now. He was probably about 12 at the time and he sat on my father's knee at that game. Like Billy, he recalls me polishing the boots the night before the game. They're the memories they would have of that All-Ireland final. They were closely involved and I'm sure their ambition was to join me on the Offaly team and maybe try and win an All-Ireland with Offaly.

'In '85 we came back to the All-Ireland final again as a very determined team. Pat Fleury captained us and we beat Galway in the All-Ireland final. It was my first All-Ireland win and it was very exciting. We also contested what, for the present generation of players, was our first senior county club final in '85. Billy was a sub that day on the club team. Also, I think in '86 Birr won the All-Ireland Colleges final and Billy was on the team that beat North Monastery in the final.

'The club also had won a couple of under-age championships and Billy, Johnny and Kieran were playing with them. That was in 1986. Offaly won the minor All-Ireland that year and Billy played in the final against Cork. In '87 Offaly came back and won the minor All-Ireland again and both Billy and Johnny played that day against Tipperary. Johnny was only 15 in that All-Ireland final. He played wing-back and was maturing very quickly. At 15 years of age, to play in an All-Ireland final was a huge achievement and I think he marked John Leahy that day. The lads were starting to come through.'

In the late 1980s the hurling careers of Joe, Billy and Johnny Dooley coalesced. By 1988 Joe was approaching 25, Billy was 19 and Johnny was almost 17. 'I think '88, at club level, would probably have been our first time to hurl together,' Joe recalls. 'We won our first-ever county championship in 1988 and we would have been scoring a lot together all during that year. Our philosophy always was to play for the team. That's how you survive, you know. If you were to go out and try to play as an individual, it wouldn't work. But we'd always follow the ball and throw the ball around and try to help one another out. That was always the simple philosophy we stuck to.'

By the early 1990s all three family members had transferred their scoring talents to the county's various hurling sides. Johnny was showing his prowess in Offaly's march to the 1989 All-Ireland minor championship. Both Johnny and Billy also were shining for the county U-21 side, with Johnny appearing in the 1989, '91 and '92 U-21 All-Ireland finals and Billy accompanying him in the '89 decider. All that time big brother Joe was an established member of the senior side.

Soon all three were together with the Offaly seniors, where they provided headaches for opposing defences. Johnny was known for his artistry and style, becoming a brilliant point-scorer from frees and from play. Billy's instinct was in netting goals, especially when they were urgently needed. Joe also racked up the goals and the points. Not surprisingly, all three brothers shared in Offaly's National Hurling League victory in 1991. Within a few more years the three Dooleys were also on their way to All-Ireland senior success.

The 1994 All-Ireland final featured the three Dooley brothers playing together in the Offaly colours. That day, Joe, Billy and Johnny emulated the Rackards and the Bonnars as they marched on to Croke Park for the match against Limerick. It was, by any standards, a curious contest. Victory for Offaly came after an extraordinary comeback. With five minutes to go Limerick led by five points. Inspired by a Johnny Dooley goal, however, Offaly won by six points. For the first time in history three family members, while all playing in the forwards, had secured All-Ireland senior success.

'There was a lot of pressure on that game because we had played so well up to the final,' Joe says. 'As regards Billy, Johnny and myself, we just thought of it as another game. I suppose history was being made but we weren't thinking about it that way. We kept our philosophy fairly simple, that we were part of a team and we were working for the team. That's the way to do it.

'On the day itself Limerick were on song for most of the game. I think we were slow to get out of the blocks and we just kept in touch. All through the game it looked as though Limerick were going to win it. I suppose Johnny's goal, with five or six minutes to go, really turned the game. Pat O'Connor followed it up with another one and then I think we scored five points in the last few minutes. I think Limerick were shell-shocked.

'It was absolutely brilliant to be part of an All-Ireland winning team with the three of us playing together. It was an emotional time. I suppose all through the year we hadn't really thought about it. It was only when we had achieved it that we could actually sit back and enjoy it. It was a proud time for my father as well and for my mother. My father really lapped it up for a good few months afterwards. Everyone was congratulating him and he was getting the odd pint here and there as well. He wasn't complaining. But I know he took huge pride out of it and he was a very proud man at that time.'

The following year the three Dooleys were back for their second All-Ireland final in a row, this time against Clare. It was a dramatic final, with the trio in the spotlight following performances that won so many plaudits all season. The match was a cracker. With minutes to go a Johnny Dooley free brought the teams level. However, two closing points from Anthony Daly and Jamesie O'Connor swung the decision for Clare. Although Offaly's fifth All-Ireland final in 15 years had come unstuck, within another three years the tables would be turned once again.

Despite losing to Kilkenny in the 1998 Leinster final, all three Dooley brothers contested that year's All-Ireland final courtesy of the newly introduced 'back door' system. After an epic three-game semi-final battle with Clare, the September All-Ireland once more paired Offaly with their Leinster final conquerors, Kilkenny. This time the affair ended well for Offaly, securing All-Ireland medals number two for Billy and Johnny, medal number three for big brother Joe. It also won for Offaly their fourth championship of the 1980s and '90s. It was an extraordinary achievement for a county of its history and size.

'There was great pride in Offaly,' Joe remarks by way of explaining the county's achievements. 'We were lucky to have enough good hurlers at the one time. Sometimes we can be hard to manage but when we all get together we can be hard to beat. We always would have looked up to the footballers in Offaly, going back to the '60s and '70s. We would have taken great inspiration from Offaly footballers. They were always known to be a team that wouldn't lie down. I think the hurlers took that up as well.

'I suppose none of us likes to be beaten and I suppose we gel together. We all got on very well, which is great. We've been away on a lot of trips and things together, so it's like a big family, really. That's probably why we're able to keep it going. Like, we won a National Hurling League in '91 and we won the All-Ireland in '98 and we probably had ten of the same team involved, eight or nine years later. There are very few counties that can boast that. The reason is that once you get involved with Offaly hurling, it's very hard to get out of it. It's harder to get off the Offaly team than it is to get on it.'

Having dominated the championship for almost two decades, Offaly hurling took a battering in the 2000 All-Ireland final. Their opponents that day were a Kilkenny side facing the prospect of three All-Ireland final defeats in a row. Having already disposed of champions Cork, Offaly's battle with their Leinster counterparts seemed likely to be a tight affair. Unfortunately for Offaly, it wasn't. On the day, a determined Kilkenny secured a one-sided victory by the score of 5–15 to 1–14.

Following the 2000 All-Ireland Offaly returned home to consider the future. Also considering his prospects was Joe Dooley. Joe was approaching 37 and had been involved with the Offaly seniors since 1982. He had won six Leinster senior championships, one National Hurling League, one Walsh Cup and one Oireachtas title to add to his three senior All-Irelands. With Seir Kieran, he had won four county championships. He also had won an All-Star award in 1998.

Back in 1999 Billy, although still a stylish hurler and a star in his own right, already had retired at the age of 30. Both he and Johnny had won All-Star awards in 1994 and '95. They also had shared National Hurling League, Oireachtas, Walsh Cup, Leinster and club titles. However, the team they played with was changing, time had passed by and their county was moving on to a new phase in its history.

Throughout the 1990s hurling had grown accustomed to the style of the Dooleys. They had excelled on the hurling stage, displaying remarkable skills especially in Leinster championships and All-Ireland semi-finals and finals. They also had demonstrated the fine art of forward play, particularly in the realms of scoring. However, having contributed so much to the game, especially at the sport's highest levels, by the end of 2000 a second member of the Dooley trio finally left. After almost two decades in senior inter-county hurling, Joe

Dooley, the father-figure of hurling's legendary family, decided to call it a day.

'I kind of felt I had given it enough,' Joe concludes. 'While I was still fit enough I felt maybe it was time to step aside and let in a young fellow. I got a lot out of it and I was glad I made the right decision. It wasn't an easy decision. It was a huge part of my life. I think every player experiences this when it comes to retirement time. But I had got a lot out of it and I was happy enough that I was going having done my bit.

'I'm very happy with what I've achieved and the successes we've had and the friends I've made and the trips. I have great memories and I wouldn't change one bit of it. There was a lot of sacrifices made and a lot of hardship. But you forget all that and, if I were advising any young fellow, I'd advise him to go the same road as I did.

'I have great memories. I saw nearly every part of the world. I was in Thailand, South Africa, Florida, Los Angeles, all over the world, and we had great times. You met a lot of players and you remember the great wins you've had as well. I suppose we've gone into the history books at this stage but it's not even that. It's more the satisfaction and enjoyment you get out of it. If I had my time over again, I'd do the exact same thing.

'There is a whole new generation of young Dooleys coming on now. My two sisters have kids and Billy has young fellows and Johnny has a young fellow. I've a young fellow myself. There will be a whole new generation coming in in the years to come. Who knows whether they'll be successful or not but all they can do is their best. Maybe they might be playing golf or rugby or something – but it's unlikely, though, I'd say.'

18. NICKY ENGLISH

BY ANY STANDARDS, NICKY ENGLISH HAD A MEMORABLE FIRST GAME AT CROKE PARK. THE event took place in the mid-1970s, when Nicky was barely a teenager. Representing the black and yellow of Arravale Rovers, Nicky and a bunch of Tipperary schoolboys travelled in awe to the Dublin venue. For that U-14 tournament game he played centre-forward.

That day, Nicky English achieved every young boy's dream. True, the crowd might have been sparse. The echoes of an empty Croke Park might have rung hollow. But at one stage in that game Nicky rattled the net. It was his first-ever goal at the venue. It was also a moment that this subsequent Hurler of the Year and multiple All-Star award winner would replicate on his path to All-Ireland success.

'Arravale Rovers took an U-14 team to Dublin to play a match in Croke Park,' Nicky recalls. 'I suppose it's unheard of now that an U-14 team from anywhere in the country would play there. I think it might have been organised through the Christian Brothers in Dublin and the Christian Brothers in Tipperary, however they managed it.

'I was part of that team for the day. I can't remember much about the match but I can remember scoring a goal into the Hill 16 end at one stage. That was the highlight of my day. I remember we stopped in Portlaoise on the way back. We felt we were after winning a major game. We got our bag of chips and we felt on top of the world. It's amazing the way these things last in your memory. For me, who had played little or no competitive hurling, to actually get to Croke Park and see it and then score a goal on my first day there, I'll never forget it.'

There would be plenty more opportunities for Nicky English to score goals at Croke Park but those opportunities would take some time to arrive. He grew up close to the Tipperary–Limerick border, where the prospects of a flourishing hurling career were far from encouraging. His village had no hurling tradition and with few budding hurlers around he practised his skills alone. However, he did have a father with an interest in the game. Also, the Tipperary side of 1971 was delivering inspiring victories over Limerick in the Munster final and over Kilkenny in the All-Ireland decider.

'In 1971 I would have been about eight years of age,' Nicky recalls. 'Tipperary, at the time, were in the Munster final. The match was being played in Killarney. I can vividly remember my father going to the match with a man called Jimmy Lynch. I remember being very upset at the fact that I wasn't being taken.

'I remember locking myself into a wardrobe and crying all day because I didn't get to see the match. Tipperary won on the day in one of our most famous victories in Killarney. I remember getting to see the All-Ireland final afterwards, so my tantrums obviously worked to some extent. They were my earliest memories of matches.'

Indulging his passion for hurling, Nicky English eventually played with the Abbey CBS team in Tipperary town. There he shared in the school's Croke Cup and Rice Cup battles. He also shared in a Fitzgerald Shield success over Rockwell College. In 1979 he made it to the county minor panel but was eventually culled from the squad. The following year, having established himself with the county minors, he incurred an unfortunate injury. However, as with Arravale some years before, he turned up at Croke Park where he again scored a goal, this time in Tipperary's All-Ireland minor final victory.

'The first match we played was against Cork,' Nicky recalls. 'A guy who became a great friend of mine, Ian Conroy, was given the job of marking Tony O'Sullivan, which was a very onerous task given that Tony, since he was 14 or 15, was really a high-powered player with the North Mon and with Cork. Ian thought he'd try to soften Tony O'Sullivan up but unfortunately it was my leg he softened up and he actually broke a bone in my leg in a ruckus or a mêlée. After that I missed the Munster final and there was no All-Ireland semi-final for us at the time.

'I came back for the All-Ireland final even though I wasn't really at 100 per cent. I played midfield in the minor in 1980 but I was corner-forward for the final. We played Wexford and I don't think I ever hit the ball out of my hand in the game. There was one ball that came across and I doubled on it and scored a goal. It kind of made my reputation but, if anything, my contribution to that was negligible.'

As so often happens in inter-county hurling, the evolution of a victorious senior team can be traced to earlier minor and U-21 successes. In Tipperary's case the pattern is no different. Having tasted victory in 1980, the Tipperary minors achieved further All-Ireland success in '82. Almost side by side, the U-21s completed a coveted three-in-a-row from 1979 to 1981. Taken together, the future looked good.

By 1981 Nicky English had progressed to the U-21s, where he shared in Tipperary's third success in a row. He was also on the brink of senior selection. 'In my memory the 1981 team was the best U-21 team that Tipp had,' Nicky declares. 'You'd probably end up with three or four All-Stars on that particular team.' Despite such talent, however, the seniors took time to evolve. Their famine, stretching back to 1971, wasn't over yet.

'I think it's unrealistic to expect young fellows to come and win an All-Ireland,' Nicky says. 'Latterly I've often heard Babs Keating and Donie Nealon say that it's difficult for an un-medalled panel to win an All-Ireland. Having people on the panel who have actually played in an All-Ireland final and won medals is very important. At that time Tipp had been unsuccessful in the championship in any shape or form for a long time. By the time we came on the senior team in 1982 they hadn't won a game since 1973. That put huge pressure on everybody associated with Tipperary teams.

'We were thrown in at the deep end in 1982. I think we had ten U-21s on the senior team that went to play Cork. We felt that we had a chance of winning but looking back on it we had absolutely no chance of beating what was a seasoned Cork team. A team needs to learn. You don't actually walk out in the senior competition and take over and win in your first year. Rarely do you do that and I've never seen it happen.'

By the mid-1980s it was clear that something special was required to ignite Tipperary and in 1986 the catalyst arrived in the form of Babs Keating. A former Hurler of the Year and All-Ireland winner, Babs was a charismatic figure whose fame and legend had taken hold in Tipperary hurling. The appointment was greeted with optimism and joy. Joined by selectors Donie Nealon and Theo English, the new management team combined leadership and experience with a modern management style. It seemed that Tipperary's famine years might end at last.

'Babs is a larger-than-life personality,' Nicky says. 'He's not prepared to take second-best in anything, in his job, in life. He was prepared to put his neck on the line for that particular group of Tipperary players and say: "Right, you're a Tipperary player. This is the way I'm going to treat you. I'm going to make you feel that you're wanted. You have a uniform, you have a badge. But I'm going to expect in return that you're going to do this, this and this for me and you're going to play like a Tipperary player of my era, the '60s."

'When he spoke to us he wasn't putting the pressure of old on us but saying that we were as good as any of these guys in the '60s and he wanted us to play like that. We didn't know what the era was like because we never saw it anyway. But straightaway there was an expectation from everybody and an expectation of ourselves. Certainly it made a huge impact. He was able to pull the thing together.

'Instead of going to matches in a minibus we were now staying overnight the night before. We had blazers, the best of gear. We had hurleys, we had everything that you wanted to perform at your best. But because of that you had to perform at your best. That really was the start of the Babs era, which was five Munster championships, two All-Irelands and two leagues over the following seven or eight years.'

Lift-off occurred in 1987 with Tipperary's victory in the Munster final. The Cork v Tipperary contest was looked forward to with great expectation. Some 60,000 supporters assembled in Thurles. That day, Nicky English scored a stunning goal slotted home with his boot past the advancing Ger Cunningham. Having drawn the first match, Tipperary were victorious after extra time in the replay in Killarney. It was Tipperary's first Munster championship in 16 barren years.

'It had been a long time since Tipperary won the Munster final,' Nicky agrees. 'Certainly the county celebrated like never before. Babs was constantly impressing on the team that they must concentrate on the All-Ireland semi-final. But you must remember that the team manager speaks to an inter-county hurling team on average three times a week. He never speaks for longer than two or three minutes. If Babs is talking to us for nine minutes a week, then that's as much as he's doing.

'Everybody else, in every village, is saying what a great win it was and that it was the time of their lives they had in Killarney. You can't stop it. You can try all you like but you can't. We were unprepared against Galway in the semi-final in '87. Having said that, we played well and Galway were a better team than people gave them credit for. Galway were a super team. Then in '88 everybody said that this is the year Tipp are going to come back and get their own back on Galway.'

In 1988 Tipperary inched closer to All-Ireland success when they not only won another Munster final against Cork but also made it to the September decider in Croke Park. For Nicky English it was a controversial occasion. Following the surprise dropping of captain Pa O'Neill, Nicky was bestowed with the honour of leading the team. The decision generated bitterness and resentment, although it hardly affected the outcome of the match against Galway. That day, Galway beat Tipperary by 1–15 to 0–14.

'There was a lot of bad feeling,' Nicky recalls. 'I was playing in my first All-Ireland and it was something I dreamt of all my life. Ultimately, it wasn't the best lead into it and instead of really looking forward to it I was a little apprehensive. There were a lot of things going on around it that annoyed me. I felt it had nothing to do with me but certainly people criticised me for it. It didn't take from the pressure of playing in it, which is enough in itself. To me, it added to it. When I look back now, it wasn't the most pleasant time for me before the match.

'The game itself passed me by. I was poor on the day. The Tipp team didn't really play very well but maybe we played as well as we were left to play because Galway at that stage were at the height of their powers. They had lost their few All-Irelands in 1985 and '86 and were really ready in '87 and '88. They had their experience of being in an All-Ireland final, which we didn't have. All these things add up. On the day, I thought Galway were clearly the better team and deserved to win.'

Had the 1989 final been lost, it would have been the first decade in GAA history in which Tipperary had failed to win an All-Ireland. The urgency to succeed was added to by the nature of Tipperary's All-Ireland opponents. Although Antrim beat Offaly in the semi-final, they were hardly looked on as a formidable hurling power. Events on the day proved that hypothesis right. Helped on by Nicky's personal tally of 2–12, which is the highest individual score in an All-Ireland final, Tipperary won by 4–24 to 3–9. The disappointments of the previous years were at last laid to rest.

'You learn more from losing any game than you do from winning a game,' Nicky reflects. 'The 1988 All-Ireland final really drove home to us that now this thing was becoming serious. For Antrim, they couldn't have been playing a worse team. Here we were having lost in '88. We had met the President; we had done all that. We had got carried away with all that before. Here we were now to accomplish and finish off a mission that had started, for some of us, seven or eight years before.

'Antrim were the team that we were the previous year, on the crest of the wave, coming in on a high, and their supporters were unused to it. They themselves were unused to it. But for us it was a case of forgetting about the national anthem, forgetting about all the trappings. Get this ball in, get this job accomplished, breathe a sigh of relief and it was relatively easy in the end.'

As they faced into 1990 Tipperary hurling was back in the sunshine and the future looked rosy. The previous year Nicky English was awarded the honour of Hurler of the Year. He also won his sixth All-Star award. The team he played with were All-Ireland champions, helped in no short measure by his ability to score important goals and points. Yet, despite scoring another goal in the 1990 Munster final, Tipperary were shocked by a hungry Cork. The team's hopes of retaining their Munster and All-Ireland trophies were shattered.

There was more left in this Tipperary team, however, as the following year would prove. In the championship they beat Limerick and eventually squeezed past Cork in a replay in the Munster decider. They then added the scalp of Galway in the semi-final before achieving their second All-Ireland success by defeating Kilkenny. The sweet taste of the '60s was back in Tipperary hurling.

'In 1991 we were on the back foot again,' Nicky says. 'In general, in Tipperary hurling we're better on the back foot. When we're favourites we're poor. We have an ability in Tipperary, amongst supporters, team players and those associated with the team, to delude ourselves into thinking that we are a great team. As we showed in 1991, we're better off on the back foot.

'We played Limerick and we played Cork in what I consider as two of the greatest games that were ever played. Then we went on and beat Galway and subsequently Kilkenny in the All-Ireland final, luckily on the day but ultimately winning against the head. That was more satisfying, if you like, given that we had beaten all the aristocrats on the way, which we hadn't done in '89.'

The problem with success is that it creates expectations and in Tipperary expectations were high at the top of the 1990s. Munster championships, All-Irelands, league finals, trips to Croke Park, homecomings and defeats of the great hurling powers were potent persuaders. Supporters demanded success. The county expected the best. Another Munster title in 1993 and a league title in 1993–94 helped sustain the illusion. But an illusion it was, as the seeds of decline were already apparent.

'Any team has only a finite life, maybe four or five years,' Nicky explains. 'If you take the life of that particular team, it really had begun in 1987 and then got the injection of new blood in the form of John Leahy and Declan Ryan in '88. It won in 1991. In 1992 it was on the rebound of a winning year and didn't really do things correctly. So by 1993, '94, '95 its life was six or seven years. It was six or seven years of age.

'At that stage, people are becoming 27, 28, 29 years of age. People are getting married, they have businesses to run, their bodies are breaking down a little bit. The bulk of them have two All-Ireland medals. They're saying: "I'm not prepared to put in the same effort as I have all my life." Maybe the management isn't as driven as it was. So looking back it's easy to see why we weren't winning. But when you're actually in there, you're saying: "We can win this any time we put our minds to it." But everybody didn't put their minds to it at the same time.

'On the day you win an All-Ireland it seems a simple thing to do. But to actually start at the bottom of the hill and win it, a lot of things need to go right. The team certainly needs experience. It needs a lot of experience but mostly bad experiences. Good experiences take the hunger off people and they become a little softer. If they have more bad experiences than good experiences then they're likely to be hungry. Ultimately, that last yard is all down to hunger and All-Irelands are won by hunger and desire. In my experience, nothing beats hunger and desire. If you have that hunger and desire, plus experience, then you're going to be very hard to beat. But going into those years the bad experiences were too far back in our memories.'

By the mid-1990s the rigours and demands of top-flight hurling were taking their toll on Nicky English. Calf strains, hamstrings and other injuries were curtailing his performances, while the first hints of a loss of speed were beginning to appear. He was, he says, spending more time in physiotherapy than on the training ground. 'I had played 13 or 14 years at that stage, so your body does start to break down. I don't know whether I suffered more than most but there were games that I would have loved to have played in but I missed.'

In 1996, after 15 years playing for his county, Nicky English retired. He was far from finished with Tipperary, however, returning as manager in the late summer of 1998. Under his stewardship they reached the Munster final in 2000, only to be beaten by Cork. The following year, with a mixture of seasoned pros and young hurlers, they achieved All-Ireland success.

'We started with a lot of young kids who really were hungry to win, interspersed with some older guys,' Nicky remarks. 'Going back to the point made by Donie Nealon and Babs, we still had players who had All-Ireland medals, such as Declan Ryan and John Leahy. Their contribution to the next victory in 2001 was immense. It was very satisfying ultimately to win the All-Ireland. Having said that, there were days when I said to myself: "Why did I ever get myself into this hole?" It felt like being in a hole, to be honest with you.

'As a coach or a manager of any sporting team, the day you win you share somewhat in the glory, although not a lot, as the credit ultimately goes to the players. That's only rightfully so because they're the people who actually win it. But on the day that they get beaten, ultimately the coach takes the hammer for that. It's difficult and, to be honest with you, it's not a nice job. But I suppose somebody has to do it.'

Every era needs a superstar and Nicky English certainly filled the role. A hurler of exceptional talent, few players caught the eye or imagination in quite the same way. He had all the attributes of stardom: skill, speed, acceleration, style and the ability to produce magic moments. Like all great players, he also produced memorable scores at crucial junctures in vital games. Many of his scores, including his remarkable 'bender' with his boot against Cork in 1987, have entered the realms of folklore. Others, including his tally of 2–12 against Antrim, are remembered as evidence of his prolific eye for goal.

Nicky blossomed during Tipperary's rise in the 1980s and was past his peak as decline set in again in the 1990s. His primacy in the '80s was reflected in three successive All-Stars from 1983 to 1985. He won three more from 1987 to 1989, including the ultimate accolade of Hurler of the Year. He was, without doubt, one of the shining stars of his county's revival in the late '80s and early '90s, winning five Munster championships, two All-Irelands and two National Hurling Leagues. Without him, it's unlikely that Tipperary's rise, had it happened at all, would have reached quite the same heights.

'Wherever I am today, or whatever I am in life, hurling has played a major part in it,' Nicky concludes. 'I've had my ups and downs along the way, probably more downs than ups. In sport, you can't win all the time. I played for 15 years and we only won twice. But at the end of it I wouldn't swap it for anything. I've enjoyed every second of it. I've met people all over the country, people I've been friendly with at UCC and in Cork. It has helped me make friends all over the place. You become part of a hurling family. It's only as you get older that you realise that most hurling people in every county have the same ambitions and the same sets of values as well.

'No matter where you're from, there's a sense of place. If you have that sense of place, then if you're brought up in Offaly one of the greatest things you can achieve is actually to play for Offaly. Where I'm coming from, I thought I never would have a chance to play for Tipperary. To actually achieve that, whether we won or lost, just putting on the Tipperary jersey at any stage, and even seeing it now, to me is really a sense of my place, my home, and I'm proud of it.'

19. BRIAN WHELAHAN

BUT FOR A LAST-MINUTE CHANGE OF HEART, OFFALY'S BRIAN WHELAHAN MIGHT NEVER have witnessed the greatest honour of his hurling career – his accession to hurling's prestigious Team of the Millennium. To be selected at all was the ultimate dream of any hurler, past or present. To be the only hurler chosen who was still playing the game, the honour of joining Ring, Mackey, Keane, Rackard and the Doyles, amongst others, was almost beyond comprehension.

Yet, as the twentieth century came to a close, this Birr-born, double All-Ireland winning hurler almost missed the great event. Worse still, his father, mentor and greatest supporter, Pat Joe Whelahan, who was an ever-present for his son's greatest moments, never made it at all. The event in question was An Post's long-awaited announcement of the game's finest, chosen from a century of hurling legends.

'I got a phone call on a Friday from an An Post representative asking would I attend a function on the Monday,' Brian recalls. 'I knew the millennium team was going to be announced and I thought that what they wanted was maybe to get a few of the current players up to Dublin and mix them in with any of the winners who were still alive. We were playing Derry the day before it, so I didn't fancy driving to Dublin on the Sunday, driving home and then going back up on the Monday.

'We played Derry and for long periods they took the game to us. Only for Johnny Dooley that day, we were in big trouble. We were a little bit down after the game. I remember coming home to Birr that evening and saying: "I'm not going to Dublin." We had a few drinks that night, analysing our performance, and my father said he'd travel up with me the following day.

'I woke up the next morning and I was a bit sore after the game and tired and feeling a bit sorry for myself. I said to my wife: "Mary, I'm not too pushed. Sure, it'll be grand, they won't miss me." She said: "You'll be whingeing and crying later on in the day if you don't go, you'll be the worst in the world." I said: "Come on then, we'll go." I called down for my father at around quarter to ten. I was to be there in Croke Park at twelve and he was a bit shook up himself. He said to go ahead, that he'd go up and help clean up around the pub.

'We drove up, took our time and we arrived in to Croke Park three-quarters of an hour late. They were going through the team selection and they had got to midfield. I think they were on Jack Lynch. They were reading out a bit about Jack's career and Micheál ÓMuircheartaigh had yarns to tell. I came in off the lift and I think the first guy I met was Seán O'Leary. He shook my hand and congratulated me and I said: "For what?" He said: "You're after being selected on the Team of the Millennium."

'I said: "Oh, Christ." I didn't expect any of this. I tried to slip in anonymously and, next thing, Christy Ring's portrait was unveiled. I'm saying to myself: "Christ, I'm up here with these lads." I sat down at a table with Ray Cummins and his wife and Jimmy and John Doyle. We had a lovely lunch and listened to the different speakers. It was very special to be there and to have received such an award. And to think I wasn't even going to travel!

'I rang my father on the way home, or he rang me, and what he didn't say to me on the phone! "Why didn't you ring me?" I said I didn't know. He was giving out. He said: "Who were you sitting beside?" I said: "I was sitting beside Jimmy Doyle and Ray Cummins, and Eddie Keher was beside us as well." "Sure, I hurled against them all . . ." I came back to the pub and he was giving out to me again. I said: "It was your own fault you didn't come. I called for you, you know."

'But it was very special. It was special to be picked and to be the only current player. That was a huge talking point in itself because if anyone was going to be picked I presumed it was going to be D.J. But when I sat down and thought about it I was delighted from an Offaly point of view. It meant that Offaly were getting an accolade for their last 20 years. What they had given to hurling over the last 20 years, the skill and the way they played the game, was getting acknowledged. It was sort of an Offaly award rather than just a personal award and that made it more special.'

From Offaly's first-ever Leinster senior hurling title in 1980 to the end of the century, no other county more consistently dominated hurling than the Faithful County. Traditionally the also-rans of Leinster, Offaly's historic provincial championship victory over Kilkenny in 1980 signalled the arrival of a new hurling force. That victory declared Offaly's resolve to emerge from the shadows of Leinster giants, Kilkenny and Wexford.

For the next 20 years Offaly's success exceeded everyone's wildest expectations. Within two decades their senior hurlers made seven trips to Croke Park to contest All-Ireland finals. They won a remarkable four of those finals, in 1981, '85, '94 and '98. Adding to Kilkenny's and Wexford's new-found woes, Offaly also swept through Leinster, winning six provincial titles in the 1980s while continuing the trend in the 1990s. With just two previous All-Ireland junior titles in the 1920s, the remarkable transformation of Offaly hurling was complete.

'Offaly really came on the scene in 1980 with their first Leinster trophy,' Brian says. 'Beating Kilkenny caused a revolution in Offaly hurling. There were only 8,000 people at the Leinster final. No one gave Offaly any hope that day yet they came away winners. It sparked a huge interest in hurling in the county, especially down around Birr where, along with Tullamore, hurling is probably at its strongest.

'To achieve the ultimate success in Leinster was never even dreamed of. Every kid in the county, especially down in south Offaly, was going around with a hurley in their hand. Clubs really got their act together. That success Offaly had in the 1980s brought on a whole new bunch of young guys who really worked hard at under-age level along with their mentors. We reaped the rewards in the 1990s.

'The way forward was obviously to promote under-age hurling in the county. That came to fruition in 1986 when both the community school in Birr and the vocational school in Banagher won their respective competitions outright. We had the basis of a very, very good minor team to pick from both schools. We won our first minor All-Ireland in '86, which ensured the continuity of hurling in the county for the bones of ten years. In '87, with a number of the '86 team, we were lucky enough to win it again.

'I happened to be part of the '87 team. It was great to hurl in Croke Park for the first time in '87 and to go on and be part of a team that won the minor All-Ireland later that year. It was just something fantastic and something no one ever dreamed of. We were after doing two in a row in minor, which was very hard for a county that had never won a minor up until 1986. Things looked good. It was a very rosy and healthy period for Offaly under-age hurling at the time.'

A glance at the team-sheets of the victorious Offaly minors in the 1980s reveals much about the state of hurling in the county. The minor championship-winning sides of 1986, '87 and '89 included the soon-to-be-familiar names of Joe Errity, Johnny Dooley, Johnny Pilkington, John Troy, Hubert Rigney, Jim Troy, Billy Dooley, Brendan Kelly, Declan Pilkington, Michael Duignan and, of course, Brian Whelahan. All those players would filter through to win All-Ireland senior medals in the 1990s.

Put quite simply, the Offaly selectors dealt with a depressingly limited pool of hurling talent in the county. For a start, take the small size of the county relative to the traditional hurling super-powers. Add in Offaly's parallel fascination with, and success in, Gaelic football. Then consider the restricted parts of the county dedicated to hurling and you get some idea of how severely curtailed the available hurling talent was.

'Hurling is probably at its strongest with all the senior clubs within ten miles of Birr, bar for, we'll say, Tullamore. To pick up such a talented bunch of players from such a small pick is very rare. We were very lucky at the time to be able to call on players like the John Troys, the Johnny Pilkingtons, the Joe Erritys, the Johnny Dooleys, the Billy Dooleys. To have such talent at our disposal doesn't happen too often in this county because we don't have the pick of the likes of Dublin, Cork, Galway or Tipperary.

'From the point of view of our own geographic structure within the county, the populated area is a football area. The mainstay of the population is from Kilcormac up, which is the predominantly football area of Offaly. The pick you have from the hurling end, I suppose, would amount to 15,000 or 20,000 people, which wouldn't even cover half the population of Cork city. We have ten or twelve senior clubs. There are more clubs in North Tipperary than there are in Offaly.

'When you look at Offaly you really have maybe a third of the population to pick from, from a hurling point of view. The rest is football. We also have one of the smallest populations in the country. We hit on a very golden period at that time and we were just very lucky. Obviously, the work that was done at primary school level, in schools around the county, and in secondary school, paved the way for the success at minor age and on into senior.

'Because we have such a small pick, it also means that just because you play wing-back for your county it doesn't necessarily mean you're going to play wing-back for your club. Joe Errity sort of made his way onto the Offaly team by playing in the forward line yet he was our club centre-back and full-back, and a very good one at that. But he had to adapt to get onto the team in the forward line.

'The same with Michael Duignan. Michael Duignan was probably the most versatile player that we ever had, playing from everywhere in the forward line and midfield for his club to playing at wing-back later for his county. At the time, hurlers in Offaly were very versatile and they were played in a lot of positions to fill gaps. We were very lucky to have such players around.'

No player epitomised the style, determination and versatility of Offaly hurling in the 1990s more than their star half-back Brian Whelahan. Few could doubt his pedigree, given his father Pat Joe's immersion in Offaly hurling and the talent of his brothers, Simon and Barry, at the game. Combining an easy command of defence with an astonishing ability to read a game, Brian was, according to his manager Michael Bond, 'the heart and soul of the team'. Captain of the successful minors in 1989, he moved straight into the senior team where he showed a cool head cleaning up at the back.

Recognised for his customary exploits at right half-back, Brian was equally talented and prolific as a forward, which was something he would later demonstrate in the 1998 All-Ireland final. It was back in 1991, however, that he tasted his first senior success while sharing in Offaly's first-ever National Hurling League title. The following year he picked up his first All-Star award. In 1994 he was sharing in Offaly's breathtaking All-Ireland victory over Limerick, having beaten Kilkenny, Wexford and Galway along the way.

'That year, 1994, was a year that was over before we realised we were All-Ireland champions,' Brian recalls. 'That was Éamonn Cregan's second year with the county. We had an awful lot of talent in the squad. It was a matter of harnessing that talent and bringing it to a head. We really had to peak for our first game against the double All-Ireland champions, Kilkenny. They were going for three in a row and if we didn't put it together for that day we were gone. There was no "back door" that time and we just had to perform. Thankfully we got it together in June and we went through.

'We still weren't seen as a major threat to proven teams at the time, like the Tipperarys, the Corks or the Galways that had contested previous All-Irelands. We were plodding along nicely and we played Wexford in the Leinster final. We played quite well and got over that comfortably enough. But we were still no major All-Ireland contenders.

'We played Galway in the All-Ireland semi-final and for 60 minutes of the game we played very good hurling. Galway came back very strong at us. It looked at one stage as if they might just pip us and go ahead. But we rallied again and we finished comfortable winners by six points. We found ourselves in an All-Ireland final and there were only two people who had played in the All-Ireland finals before and they were Jim Troy and Joe Dooley. It was a very young and inexperienced team from that point of view.

'We were playing Limerick, who were in very much the same boat as ourselves. The one thing we had on Limerick was that we had Éamonn Cregan training us. It was a very hard position that he found himself in because he would have trained a lot of these guys at U-21 level and up along. He obviously had an insight to their hurling, their type of hurling and the type of players they were. That was a big help for us, although it probably didn't look like that early in the game.

'Limerick came in that year very fit, very eager and very hungry. For, I suppose, 60 minutes of the game they looked as if they were going to pick up the cup. But we probably got a lucky break with Johnny Dooley's goal. He went for it and I think it caught the defenders and the goalkeeper by surprise. That just seemed to set the ball in motion and from there the way it finished will probably never be repeated again.

'To score 2–6 in five minutes is just something that fairytales are made of and the year was over before we realised we were All-Ireland champions. It was something we never expected at the start of the year. We set out to beat Kilkenny; that was our big thing. Anything after that, like winning a Leinster title, would have been probably a great first step for us. But to finish with an All-Ireland was something no one ever dreamed of in '94.'

In the wake of the 1994 All-Ireland final Brian Whelahan's career with his club and county blossomed. In subsequent years he won county and All-Ireland club championships with Birr, shared in Offaly's All-Ireland final loss to Clare in 1995, tasted further success in the Leinster championship and was voted Man of the Match on more occasions than anyone can remember. His rise in the game was also marked by his selection as Hurler of the Year in 1994 and 1998.

Also, contrary to expectations, Brian and his Offaly team-mates were back at the 1998 All-Ireland final, having lost to Kilkenny in the Leinster final. Working their way through the 'back door', they luckily emerged from a semi-final replay brought about when the referee ended the first game two minutes early with Offaly three points in arrears. Then who else should they face in the final but their near-neighbours and template for hurling success, Kilkenny!

That All-Ireland final day in Croke Park Brian Whelahan delivered one of the finest performances of his hurling career. Despite suffering from flu, he started in defence and was later shifted to the forwards. There he delivered a devastating display, scoring 1–6 in a performance that will undoubtedly stand the test of time. The most influential player on the field, his display that day will long be remembered.

'We were probably very much even-favourites with Kilkenny going into that game. Kilkenny had beaten us quite comfortably in the Leinster final but, as we all know, we had a change of management and Michael Bond brought new, fresh ideas to the squad. There was a little bit more hunger in us, in the fact that we wanted to prove people wrong. We wanted to go out and give our best.

'In the final we didn't start as promisingly as we had hoped but we were well there come half-time. From my own point of view, I knew I wasn't on my game early on even though I got the first ball into my hand and cleared it and made a couple of other clearances. I just knew I was a little bit off. In fairness, the selectors saw that quite early on and responded to it by moving me up front.

'That gave me time to get a bit of a breather and it meant that the team wasn't conceding easy scores. It gave the back line a chance to regroup and tighten things up, which they did magnificently. When I got the first score in the first half from play, it settled me. I said: "Right, you have to make the best of this now." And it just went on from there.

'At half-time I was switched to full-forward. That was a big move for me, to go in on Pat O'Neill, because I never even dreamed of it. To be facing someone like Pat O'Neill is a very daunting task because he's such a big, strong man and he commands the area with a lot of power and respect. I was just hoping that things would go right and you couldn't have asked for them to go any better.

'I think it was the one performance of all the performances that Offaly gave in All-Ireland finals. People said Offaly hurled well and that's always nice to hear. It was the first time anyone had won an All-Ireland through the "back door" and the whole county was celebrating for the weeks surrounding it. By going on and winning it, things went through the roof. We really enjoyed ourselves for a few months. The '98 final definitely will never be forgotten as a classic in Offaly.'

But for a few twists of fate Offaly might well have contested the next All-Ireland final, against Kilkenny, in 1999. As it happened, they lost to Cork in a thrilling semi-final contest, having missed a vital free at a critical juncture of the match. In the game's closing stages Offaly's ageing team succumbed to a youthful Cork side coached by Jimmy Barry-Murphy. It seemed that Offaly's hurling honeymoon might well be coming to a close.

Contrary to expectations, Offaly reversed the result in the 2000 semi-final when they caught by surprise an over-confident Cork. However, few could have predicted the subsequent drubbing they would receive from Kilkenny in the September All-Ireland decider. Facing each other for the second time in three years, Kilkenny hammered Offaly by 5–15 to 1–14 in one of the most one-sided All-Irelands in decades. It was a day for the Careys, Shefflins and Carters, not for the Whelahans, Pilkingtons and Dooleys.

'Nothing went right for us on the day,' Brian reflects. 'I think we all felt we had a very good chance against Kilkenny in the final. We were starting to hurl a little bit better as the year went on. We overcame Cork, which a lot of people said was a great game. It wasn't a fantastic game of hurling but I don't think Cork minds were right going in on the day. I felt we were starting to improve and we might lift ourselves one last time for Kilkenny. But it didn't happen.

'We needed to hold Kilkenny for 25 minutes or half an hour into the game before they got a goal. We had to keep the pressure on them. That didn't happen. Kilkenny got the start they had wished for and that was to get a goal in the first two minutes. It was a disaster from our point of view. It just set Kilkenny up for the day that they had ahead of them. It took the whole pressure of losing three All-Ireland finals off their shoulders immediately. You could nearly see the pressure lift off their shoulders and they were able to express themselves.

'Contrary to what a lot of people say, for the remaining 20 minutes of the first half we actually hurled quite well. We were ten points down after about twelve minutes. We brought it back to five and we had a glorious chance of a goal. It just sneaked by the post and went wide. If we scored that goal, there were only two points in it just before half-time. It would have been a huge lift for Offaly.

'But we missed the goal. They came out and got their third goal and, instead of being just two points down, we were now eight points. They finished on a high with two quick points before half-time. The game was effectively over. We came back from ten and eleven points down against Clare but the way Kilkenny were hurling that was never going to happen.

'It was very disappointing for us because it was possibly the main break-up of that team of the '90s. It was disappointing to go out on that note. I won't say there was another All-Ireland in that team, but there was definitely a better performance than what we showed on the day against Kilkenny. From that point of view, it was just disappointing.'

With his selection on the Team of the Millennium to prove it, Brian Whelahan stands alone as the exceptional right half-back of all time and the finest hurler of the 1990s. Of all his contemporaries, he alone joined legends from the past in the century's élite hall of fame. His style and command in defence marked him out among his peers. His inspirational presence also helped drive an Offaly team to success way beyond their wildest expectations.

Like most great athletes, Brian Whelahan found his niche at the right time and in the right place. Inspired by the Offaly hurlers of the 1980s and coached to perfection, Brian and a rare combination of team-mates pushed out the limits for their clubs and county. In doing so, alongside great players like Johnny Pilkington, Johnny Dooley, John Troy and Joe Dooley, Brian Whelahan helped define an era in Offaly hurling that may take some time to repeat.

'It was a golden era in Offaly hurling and it's something you mightn't see again,' Brian concludes. 'It's very important that it doesn't go back to pre-1980. It's very important that doesn't happen. I think it's important for the GAA that counties like Offaly don't just fade away into the background. The Offalys, the Clares, the Wexfords have given great excitement to the GAA hurling world and it's very important that you don't have just the one set of teams in it year after year.

'We had a good spell for 20 years, make no mistake, but it's very important we don't just drift away into the background. That's all anyone can ask for. I'm not saying we're going to have such a dominant period again but if we're there or thereabouts with a decent team, we will pick up our share of titles. That's all we're looking for.'

20. D.J. CAREY

THE PROBLEM CHOOSING HURLING HEROES IN KILKENNY HAS ALWAYS BEEN THE SHEER number to pick from. Whatever the decade, the selection is vast. At no time was that more true than in the 1970s and early '80s. Nine All-Ireland finals with six victories in thirteen years provided fertile images for young boys and girls. Great names dominated Kilkenny hurling: Eddie Keher, Noel Skehan, Frank Cummins, Fan Larkin, Kieran Purcell, Pat Delaney, Billy Fitzpatrick and Ger Henderson. Hurlers like that generate potent dreams and hopes; they also engender future Kilkenny stars.

If you were born in 1970, as D.J. Carey was, then you landed right in the heart of those glory years. By the age of nine you were celebrating your fourth All-Ireland title. As you entered your teens your heroes were winning a further brace of championship victories. Add in a natural aptitude for sport, an uncle with an interest in hurling and a secondary education at the famous hurling academy, St Kieran's College, and the chances are that you will gravitate to sport, perhaps even to hurling.

'I used to come home from school and the bag was thrown in the corner,' D.J. Carey recalls. 'I'd start hitting balls against the gable-end of the house. I was Eddie Keher coming from ten goals and ten points down in an All-Ireland final, winning the match with ten minutes to go. I never saw Eddie play but obviously he was the huge name at that time. He was the name on everybody's lips. You modelled yourself on or idolised someone at that stage and Ger Henderson was my hurling hero because he was someone I grew up with.

'My Uncle Martin hurled with a local club here and he used to bring us to all the matches. I have three brothers and three sisters but the three brothers are all fairly close to one another in age, so we used to travel with him. There was a granduncle of mine, Paddy Phelan, who was on the national Team of the Century and the Team of the Millennium, and he was obviously a great man in his day. That's going back to the '30s. Also, an aunt of mine, Peggy Carey, was on four All-Ireland camogie winning teams with Kilkenny. We had those to follow as players.

'That developed on to school level. We had two great teachers in national school, John Knox and Dick O'Neill, and I can remember running home from school every day with the hurley, solo-running with the ball. If it was the hurling season you were running home with the hurling ball. If it was the football season then it was the football. You'd throw the bag in the corner and you'd hit a ball against the wall until it would get dark.

'The Kerry footballers were also an influence over me as a youngster. I grew up with that Kerry team and when I had a choice of playing either hurling or football for Kilkenny at U-12 level I actually chose football. I wanted to be a footballer, not realising what Kilkenny football was like.'

It didn't take long for D.J. Carey to recognise that Gaelic football and Kilkenny didn't quite fit together. Having played football for his county at U-12 level, he eventually gravitated to the more popular hurling code. Naturally small in stature and still growing, he played in goal at club level, which probably cost him a place with the 1987 Kilkenny hurling minors. 'I was so small that I was a keeper,' D.J. recalls. 'I was put in goal by my own club, who were intermediate at the time. I was playing in goal since I was 15. That meant I was going for the minor Kilkenny goal and I wouldn't have had much of a chance of that. If I was getting a trial for out the field I would have had a chance.'

There was never any doubt that D.J. Carey would eventually excel at sport. From the moment he moved to St Kieran's College his natural talent and commitment to sporting pursuits marked him out as an exceptional prospect. At St Kieran's he played many sports including hurling, Gaelic football, soccer and handball. In time, however, his interest in hurling won out.

A breeding ground for great hurlers, St Kieran's and D.J. won All-Ireland Colleges titles in 1988 and '89. He was also selected for the

Kilkenny minors in 1988, with whom he went on to All-Ireland success that year. Within two more years he had added an All-Ireland U-21 championship to his growing medal collection.

'We had a great Kilkenny minor team at that time,' D.J. reckons. 'It was backboned by Kieran's College, who were coming off a couple of senior All-Ireland titles. Kilkenny CBS were almost as strong as us at the time. We used to meet one another regularly and we used to come off best on most occasions, even though they were very strong as well. It was great.'

If a county is lucky there arrives, once in a generation, a player of flair and charisma who transcends the normal parameters of hurling greatness. From the beginning it was clear that D.J. Carey fitted the picture to perfection. Having won All-Ireland minor and college titles in 1988, he was soon joining up with the county seniors. In a county that had failed to win a senior All-Ireland in five years, such is the calibre of exceptional talent that selectors crave.

Although slight in stature and playing in a game dominated by giants, D.J. soon showed the hurling skills commensurate with Kilkenny's enormous expectations. He was fast, agile, intelligent, with deadly accuracy and a powerful shot. He exuded enormous confidence on the field of play and had the sort of star quality that is normally seen in exceptional talents like Christy Ring and Jimmy Doyle. Few could miss the buzz in the crowd as D.J. bore down on goal, his hurley held short. He was also a deadly penalty-taker, cool, assured, powerful and accurate. He was equally accurate with frees. It was just a matter of how much he would score, as far as the crowd was concerned.

Interestingly, D.J. had excelled at many sports as his early rise as a hurler took place. He used his pace playing soccer during his time at St Kieran's. 'It wasn't that I was a great soccer player but I was fast,' D.J. explains. 'They used to play me somewhere around the middle of the field. When someone got the ball they kicked it straight through and my job was to be gone, to run. I got a good few goals but I missed as many goals at soccer as I scored because the old foot wasn't the best at kicking it straight.' He also developed powerful wrists playing handball, at which, in time, he won All-Ireland titles. Those attributes of pace and strong wrists would soon become lethal components in one of the deadliest forwards in Kilkenny hurling history.

'Hurling is a wristy game,' D.J. explains. 'It's not all brawn. It's not just a big, wild swing. It's true, in many ways, that the harder and longer and bigger your swing is, the further the ball will go. But you won't have the time to do that. You shorten your hurley and you develop your wrist work. The stronger your wrist, the better.

'It's the same in most sports that handle a ball. Look at rugby: rugby is a wrist game when you're passing the ball. Golf is a wrist game. So is tennis. Any work that's being done should be done with your wrist. So obviously the shorter you can hold the hurl, the harder you can hit the ball. You're at a much better advantage because you can't be hooked from behind as easily or you can't be blocked as easily as you will be if you're winding up to hit a ball.

'There are no miracles and you can't do it overnight. It's what you've done all your life, from when you started hurling until now. I just can't go out and say I'm going to turn it on if I haven't the work done throughout the years. Most of it is probably instinctive, in some ways. But you've got to have serious fellows around you. While an individual will score and an individual will play very well on particular occasions, he won't win a match on his own without the work being done around him.

'I've often played much better hurling while not scoring a whole lot. Maybe I'm a bit harsh but a lot of people that look at the game, or that are at games, they wait for the papers the following day to see what such a fellow scored. They'll judge him by what he scored, not by what he's done in a game. I've always said that I'm better off the ball than I am at scoring. There are scorers as good as me, or better than me, on the team.

'I base the game on hard work and getting stuck in and blocking and hooking. If the score comes along, I can take it, fine. But I would never judge a fellow on what he scores. It's how many balls his man clears and how many he doesn't clear, that's what's more important because the longer the ball can be held in the forward line the better it is for everyone on the team.'

From 1991 to 1993 the legend of D.J. Carey took off in three successive All-Ireland finals. Despite D.J.'s personal tally of 0–9, Kilkenny lost to Tipperary in '91. A beautifully struck penalty by D.J. helped reverse Kilkenny's fortunes the following year, when the

Noresiders beat the Rebels in the '92 decider. Kilkenny then went on to make it two wins in a row in '93, following some inspired scoring performances by D.J. on the road to the final. He chalked up a personal tally of 2–4 against Offaly and a further 1–5 against Wexford in the replayed 1993 Leinster final. Although strangely subdued in the All-Ireland final, his team beat Galway to retain the championship.

'We had a great chance of winning in 1991,' D.J. says. 'Along the way we played Wexford. We should have been beaten that day. We played Dublin in the Leinster final and we could have been beaten the same day. Then we faced Antrim in the semi-final and it was two points in the last minute of the game that won it for us. On each of the three occasions we could have been beaten. Yet on the one day we probably should have been beaten most of all, we could have won. That was a great year. That was a great stepping-stone for us, a great learning experience.

'In 1992 we came up against Offaly en route. Offaly were hurling very well but we ran out winners in the end. We had a semi-final against Galway, a great game, and again in the end we came good. In the final it was a terrible day, an absolutely brutal day, with fierce wind and rain. We played against the wind in the first half and we only went in two points down. Kilkenny had scored a goal and two points to Cork's seven points. They had missed a few chances but anyone could miss chances on that day. It was a good day for myself obviously because of the goal and two points I got in the first half. The goal was from a penalty and the two points were from play.

'The next year then we were an even better team. Ollie Walsh was a brilliant manager, a great hurling man. He had such a bond in the dressing-room with all the players. He knew when it was time to have the *craic* and he knew when it was time to be serious. Ollie let you know if things weren't going right but he gave you credit if they were. He put a very good team together. In 1993 we played real well all year right up to the final. Even in the final we had to play well because it was Galway.

'P.J. Delaney and Adrian Ronan were the star forwards on the day. Myself, John Power and Eamon Morrissey were probably being watched fairly closely because of the damage we did all year. Ronan and Delaney came up, I think, with about a goal and three points each on the day. Delaney got a great goal with about three or four minutes to go to settle the game. They were absolutely glorious years for us, with an excellent team. The team itself broke up through no one's fault, really, but it broke up fairly quickly after that.'

Following the successes of 1992 and '93, the Kilkenny side sank into temporary decline. Despite the county's demise, over the next four years D.J., who was Hurler of the Year in 1993, continued to produce outstanding performances, winning All-Star awards in 1993, '94, '95 and '97 to add to those won in 1991 and '92. Then in 1998, with Kilkenny once more on the brink of success, D.J. shocked the sporting world by announcing his retirement from the game. His decision followed an extraordinary rash of toxic and malicious rumours concerning his personal, business and sporting life, which spread like wildfire throughout Kilkenny.

'I just felt at the time that there was too much going on around me that shouldn't have been going on. The one thing I would have no problem with, and I can't see myself ever having a problem with, is criticism. Anyone who goes on the field and plays badly, he can accept he was bad. If he has to make excuses over being bad, then he just has to look at himself. But when rumours that are not true start to go on, it's different. I was finding that I was having to defend myself with lies being told. A lot of it happens closer to home than you would think. Rumours about my business, rumours about all sorts of stuff were going on.

'It's easy to talk. But what people have got to realise is that the laugh and the joke that they get out of it, or the lies that they tell, it's hurting someone. It can hurt someone fairly badly and I felt that there was way too much of that going on. I was an amateur player getting nothing for the game. I worked hard. I had a family. I had a lot of things to defend. You're playing a sport at the highest level but you're not getting anything for it. On a Monday morning you've got to get up and go and make a living. You're travelling around the country and you're hearing stuff that's going on around you which is not true at all and a lot of it is being said by people who should not have been saying it.

'A lot of stuff was brought up that was all about the manager and myself. The same fellows who were mouthing and starting rumours were going around saying it was a problem between myself and Kevin

Fennelly. We lost the county final in 1997 but we won one the previous year. Any team can lose a county final. It was never about any one individual and myself. There was a lot of stuff the manager had absolutely nothing to do with. But there was a lot of stuff going on and then people put one and one together and got three.

'When you're a high-profile player you will get that. But, having said that, you go back and you look at it and it can make you a much stronger person. I had often thought about taking them on and then I felt "no" because by taking them on you were letting them get to you. The way I looked at it was to pull away from the situation. If they're carrying on that way, they're not worth it. Some of the people who were saying my business was not going well were the very same people who hadn't the guts to start a business themselves. If they want to criticise, let them go out and start one themselves and see how they'll get on.'

After a six-week retirement D.J. Carey returned to the Kilkenny fold in time for the 1998 championship campaign. They reached the All-Ireland final in 1998, where they lost to Offaly. The following year they faced Cork on a grim All-Ireland final day at Croke Park, where they lost a match in which D.J., surprisingly, was kept scoreless. Then in 2000, faced with a possible run of three losses in a row, they destroyed Offaly in one of the most one-sided All-Ireland finals in recent history. With a final score of 5–15 to 1–14, who was named Man of the Match, won his eighth All-Star award and, not surprisingly, was voted Hurler of the Year? Who else but D.J. Carey!

'We did not go on the field on that occasion any more determined than we were for the two previous years. The three-in-a-row was a huge media thing. Often it was said to me maybe as a sneer or a joke. But it was never once discussed in the Kilkenny dressing-room that we were going for three in a row. It was a media thing, the very same as there was pressure on me to perform in an All-Ireland final.

'There was no pressure put on me by my team or management or family, or even myself, to perform on the day. The pressure was to win an All-Ireland final. Whoever did the business on the day: if it was me, well, I got the same medal as the man beside me; if it was the man beside me then I got the same medal as him. It's as simple as that.

'It happened for us on this occasion. It didn't happen the two previous years but I cannot say that we left anything behind us in the dressing-room on the other two occasions. Our performance on the field was not good enough to beat either Offaly or Cork.

'We came out in the year 2000 and we played great. We got a good start. Every time Offaly tried to come back we got a goal. They missed a goal midway through the first half that could have turned things. But it was fantastic from our point of view because we put in an All-Ireland final performance that every team in the country who gets to an All-Ireland final would love to put in.

'You'll have some quarters saying that Offaly weren't a good opposition. Offaly were actually a great opposition. Offaly had been a great team for the previous 15 or 20 years. They'll always have the hurling but they have great spirit because once they put on an Offaly jersey they're all in it together. They were a very good team. They were All-Ireland champions in 1998, very unlucky not to be in the All-Ireland final in '99 and they were in it in the year 2000, having beaten the All-Ireland champions on the way. Nobody can say they were a bad team. It was a great performance by us on that occasion. Everything went really right for us as well and they're the occasions you love to have.'

Throughout his career D.J. Carey always spoke his mind openly while maintaining a high profile as a leading light of the Kilkenny team. Never short of newspaper column inches, he made headlines in 2000 with his endorsement of the GPA, the new Gaelic Players Association, of which he became a member and a strong supporter. In the wake of the 2000 championship the GPA announced a ten-player sponsorship deal and one of those players was D.J. Carey.

'My stand on that is if I'm presenting medals or I'm coaching kids, if I can do it, I have never asked or sought money and won't,' says D.J. 'But if there's a commercial venture out there where a company wants to make a profit on my back, in other words they want me for an opening or a golf day or whatever, then in my opinion I should be paid for that day. That's because I'm a high-profile person and every player in the country should be the same. If they're wanted for a commercial venture they should be paid for that.

'I hope the GPA is here to stay. I'm a member of it but I'm also a GAA member. I pay my subscription every year. I'm a GAA player and for me there's no better organisation in the world. But I do think the GPA is here to stay. As far as I'm concerned, the players should have their say and hopefully they'll have a stronger say in the future.'

From his early days D.J. Carey was known as 'Dodger', an appropriate description for a will-o'-the-wisp player with the talent to mesmerise defences and audiences alike. Popular with the media, he combined the pressures of modern-day hurling with the heavy training demands of the game and the running of his Gowran-based business. He was also known for his exploits with his club, Young Irelands.

He was a surprise omission from the Team of the Millennium. Despite his prolific scoring feats, his Hurler of the Year and All-Star awards, his All-Ireland medals and his inspirational role in Kilkenny hurling, he failed to make the cut in the An Post/GAA selection. On his team's return from the 2000 All-Ireland final that omission prompted a welcome-home banner in Kilkenny declaring: 'Who's on the stamp? D.J.'s on the stamp!' It was, perhaps, the ultimate hometown tribute to the outstanding forward of the modern hurling game, D.J. Carey.

'You value your victories and you value All-Irelands but you can take them for granted a little bit as well,' D.J. concludes. 'In other words, they can be put up on a shelf and put up in a corner and they may not be dusted. But I certainly would value every victory that I have had at any level, let it be county championship or Leinster championship or the league or All-Ireland. Whatever it is, I would value them all. But it's amazing, you probably take them for granted when you have them.'